An Adoption Journey

of

Faith Hope and Love

An Adoption Journey

of

Faith Hope and Love

Michelle L. White

I have tried to recreate events, locales and conversations from my memories of them. In order to maintain their anonymity, in some instances I have changed the names of individuals and places. I may have changed some identifying characteristics of individuals.

Contact:
Michellewhiteadoptionjourney@gmail.com

Cover and photograph by Michelle White

Acknowledgments

To God our Father and Jesus your son, who make all things possible, thank you for your unconditional love, and for blessing us with a family.

Anya and Haley, you have given us more than we could ever give you. I am humbled that God chose me to be your mom. I am also sorry in advance for anything I may do to screw that up! Remember that when you are 40 and talking to your therapist…I did the best I could.

Sean, thank you for sharing me with your siblings. The times we've all shared together are priceless. You also gave me the chance to be a bio-mom, an amazing gift!

Jeff and Ryan, my sons from another mother, thank you for allowing me to be such a special part of your lives. Good times!

To my husband Jeff, thank you for loving me just the way I am. I know it hasn't been easy!

We are eternally grateful to Anya and Haley's birth families for their gift of love, even if they may not have viewed it that way at the time.

Thank you to my parents, who not only raised me, but inspired me with compassion for others and for guiding me on this path.

To my in-laws, Larry and Cheryl, we are blessed by your unconditional love for our children.

To our favorite pastor and friend, Ed, your support, prayers and love for our family means the world to us.

To **all** of our friends and family, and there are a lot of you, who prayed with us, cried with us, encouraged us, and continually show your love for our kids, we could never thank you enough.

Thank you to all of the people who encouraged me to write our story!

Contents

For God and my family.

One

A Seed Planted

Someone once told me, "The children you adopt were always meant to be yours. They were just born to someone else."

People have often said to me they could never do what we did, referring to adopting a child. There are a lot of things in this world we are meant to do. We may not recognize it for a long time, but God gives us the calling and the ability to do them. Not everyone is called to do what we did, but each person has something wonderful, they too, are meant to do.

Looking back on my life and my husband's, our paths were clearly laid out to adopt. We just didn't realize it for a long time, and we took a lot of detours along the way.

My path started before I was born… It was during the time of the Korean War. My father served in the US Army. He was on a peacekeeping mission in South Korea to protect its citizens. While he served, he spent time getting to know the people who lived there. He had a great deal of compassion for them. They were poor, malnourished, and had little hope. Their homes were no more than shacks, put together with corrugated metal. Even worse, some of the children were being used by the enemy as human bombs in the war.

Years later, when his service ended he met my mom, they married and had me. During this time he never forgot those children or his desire to somehow help, even if it was just one child.

When I was about five years old my parents filed for the adoption of a baby girl from Korea. I was young, but still have a clear memory of visits by social workers and the excitement of having a new sister.

Just before the baby was to get on the airplane to come to the United States, the adoption fell through. There was a medical issue with her. It was thought she might have tuberculosis and wasn't allowed to enter the U.S. This turned out later not to be true, and she was adopted by someone else. My parents were absolutely devastated. They never again tried to adopt, or have any more children.

While I was growing up, my dad shared stories with me about the people of Korea and others around the world who were less fortunate. I would sometimes think about what it would be like to have children. At a young age, I already knew I wanted a lot of them, biologically, and adopted.

We attended church pretty much every Sunday since the day I was born. Throughout my life I had a love for God and a compassion for others…until I became a teenager. I had somehow forgotten my sense of the suffering of others, and the stories my dad shared with me.

Like a lot of kids my age, I had become self-centered, with little concern for the world around me. I even stopped going to church. My parents were beside themselves and didn't know how to deal with the person I had become.

"We're going for a ride," said my dad one Sunday afternoon. "Where?!" I exclaimed. "I have things to do. I'm not going!" I don't know why I thought this statement was going to work with my father, a full-blooded Italian man whom you did not talk back to, but I said it anyway.

Pretty soon, the three of us were in the car, heading down the freeway towards Los Angeles. I sat in the back seat, infuriated that they had ruined what was left of my weekend by taking me on some mystery excursion. I silently stared out the window, the half-hour car ride doing nothing to appease my anger.

As we drove through the heart of Los Angeles, I began to notice the homeless people sleeping on the streets. My anger slowly subsided and gave way to the compassion I once had. I knew why my parents had taken me there. The trip we took that day was unfortunately not a cure for my behavior, but it helped pave the way for what God was doing in my life.

Fast forward to my adult years…In my twenties, I married and had a son. I was also raising my two step-sons, Jeff and Ryan, whom I loved like my own. Life was good. Even though I had a biological child, and two other children whom I was raising, I never really gave up my dream to someday adopt.

One day I approached my husband with the idea. He wanted nothing to do with it. In his mind he had plenty of kids, and openly admitted he didn't think he could love someone else's child as much as his own. That didn't make him a bad person, he was being honest. Still, I was devastated, and thought somehow I could persuade him otherwise. I secretly went to adoption seminars to gather as much information as I could, in hopes I could somehow make him see how wonderful it would be.

It was to no avail. And as the years passed, the two of us grew apart due to many other issues we were battling. We eventually divorced. Not only did I grieve for our marriage, and the break-up of our family, I also grieved for the dream that I would never adopt a child.

Two

New Beginnings

I had been separated and divorced from my first husband for almost four years. Thankfully, we were able to remain friends. During this time I started going back to church. I hadn't attended much in over a decade. I was re-building a relationship with God and my life was at peace again.

One weekend, my son, Sean and I made the two hour drive from San Diego to the San Gabriel Mountain area to attend the wedding reception of my best friend, Kim. It was being held at her parent's home, who were like a second mom and dad to me. My parents and a lot of my childhood friends were there. It was great to see so many old friends. We spent the evening laughing and remembering old times.

When it was time for the traditional bouquet and garter toss, I was cajoled into this ritual by several well- meaning friends. Kim is a romantic at heart so it was no surprise that she chose the upstairs balcony from which to toss the wedding bouquet. As I watched it fly, in seemingly slow motion right towards me, I had no choice but to catch it.

When Kim's new husband, Dan, tossed the garter, at first, I couldn't see who caught it. It wasn't until it was time for the traditional dance between the two of us that I was able to see him.

I was then paired up with this handsome looking guy with a great smile. He had a bit of a boyish charm to him. His name was Jeff, and he was the best friend of the groom. Surprisingly, I hadn't met him before. At least I thought I hadn't. We found out later that we had met almost twenty years before at another wedding.

Throughout the evening Jeff and I danced and spent a lot of time talking. Sparks flew so bright, it was clear to those around us that we were already falling for each other.

When the reception was over we exchanged phone numbers. As Jeff handed me his number, it was then when my heart sank...the area code. Jeff lived in Ontario and I lived in San Diego. The two cities were about a two-hour car ride away from each other. The distance between the two of us was going to be, to use a term Jeff uses "geographically challenging." We exchanged numbers anyway.

A few days later Jeff called to ask if he could see me again. We decided to try it for one date. The next weekend he came to San Diego. We went to the beach to watch the sunset. And in the same evening drove up to the mountains to stargaze, one of my favorite things to do. We fell hard for each other.

The next two months were spent working, seeing each other on weekends, and talking on the phone for hours at a time. We knew beyond a shadow of a doubt that this relationship was meant to be. Eight weeks after we met Jeff proposed, and I said yes.

My friends at home thought I was out of my mind for wanting to marry a guy I barely knew. They didn't know any of my friends from where I grew up so they didn't understand the situation. Even though Jeff and I had never run in the same circles, he and I had a lot of mutual friends in the area. I would have heard from someone if he was a crazy person. I knew in my heart I loved Jeff, and that he was the man I was supposed to marry, and yes, maybe we both were just a little crazy.

One of the many things we talked about was where we would live. He wanted to move to San Diego, which was great news! We also talked about having children. Jeff had a son who was almost grown. I had my son, and two step-sons in my life. I had long ago put my adoption dream to rest, a dream I had never told Jeff about. I was at peace with it, and no longer had the desire to adopt. We agreed not to have any more children.

Jeff put his house on the market and requested a job transfer from his company. We were married within the year on a bluff over-looking the Pacific Ocean.

For two months Jeff and I were long-distance husband and wife. Finally, his job transfer went through, his house sold, and he was able to move. Our family seemed complete.

Shortly after we were married, that burning desire to adopt a child was back. *Where had this come from?!* I was nearly forty, adopting a child wasn't something I thought about anymore. Regardless, as time went by, the feeling kept getting stronger. I finally approached Jeff with the idea, not sure how he would take it. Surprisingly, he agreed to think about it.

As the weeks passed, the desire in me to adopt kept getting stronger and stronger. It was to the point where it was all I could think about. Jeff was silent on the issue. I knew, I could not, and would not push him into it unless it was something he absolutely wanted. Yet, I couldn't understand why God would put this on my heart and not on Jeff's. It was all so confusing.

Occasionally I would ask him if he had thought about the idea. His reply was always the same…he wasn't sure. I took it to God and prayed. I asked God, if it was His will we adopt a child, then to put it on Jeff's heart as strongly as it was on mine. If not, I prayed God would once and for all take the desire away from me, and give me peace about it.

One Sunday, not too long after I prayed that prayer, we were sitting in church. While we were waiting for service to begin I browsed through the program. It stated there would be a baby dedication. *Oh great,* I said to myself, another baby dedication. At this point, I could hardly bear these, along with baby showers and all the rest of the excitement that came with having new children. *What was going on here?!*

I thought I was okay with not having any more children, yet, it was hurting me more than ever. I did not want to be there and was actually getting angry, with whom I did not know. I thought about getting up and leaving to avoid the flow of tears that would surely follow. But we were sitting in nearly the front row and there was no escape without someone noticing. I stayed in my seat feeling guilty for being so bitter.

As the couple walked out onto the stage I noticed this baby dedication was different than the others we had been to. There were two children, and they were older. It caught my attention. The couple had just adopted these children from another country. I began to cry. It felt like my dream now belonged to someone else. I tried to stop the tears, but couldn't. I looked over at Jeff, and to my shock, he was not only crying, but sobbing hard. I reached for his hand and held it. I knew right then God was working on his heart.

I couldn't tell you what the sermon was about that day. I was too caught up in what was going through Jeff's mind. I could hardly wait for the service to end.

As we walked out of the church and into the parking lot, Jeff turned to me and said, "We need to do this!" "Are you sure?!" I asked. He said he was positive! And so began our journey…

Three

A Dream Reborn

Not too long after that Sunday in church there was an advertisement in a local San Diego magazine which caught my attention. It was an adoption seminar being held in town. It was put on by an adoption agency. I excitedly told Jeff about it, and he agreed we should check it out.

As much as I wanted to bring another child into our home it was important to see how my son felt. He was a teenager at the time. Our decision would impact his life as well. When we spoke with him about our plans he was supportive of our idea. This meant a lot to me.

We attended the meeting held by the agency. It was informative and answered a lot of our questions. This particular seminar was based primarily on Russian adoptions. The speaker handed out a checklist of the requirements made by the Russian government in order to adopt. The first one required we be married a minimum of two years. That was do-able, but meant we would have to wait about another year.

The director told us we could file for adoption before that time period; we just couldn't finalize anything until the two-year mark. The next obstacle was the rule that Russia requires two trips, in person, to their country in order to adopt. It was at this point when I leaned over to Jeff and whispered, "We aren't going to Russia, because I am *not* flying there twice."

You see, I am terrified to fly. I can't imagine it once, much less twice. I have been flying pretty much my whole life, but for some reason my fear of it has gotten worse, not better.

As the meeting concluded we felt good about this particular agency, and country, but I still wasn't sure about all of the flying we would have to do. We also wanted to check out all of our options, and different countries, before filling out an application.

Over the next several months we did a lot of research on adoption. We looked into many different places that had children available, including the United States. Each country has its own criteria for prospective parents. There were a lot of places where we didn't qualify to adopt. China preferred older parents, and no other children in the home. Kazakhstan required a six week stay in their country, which was not an option for us. Korea required a minimum of a five year marriage. I was sad about that one. I had always thought I would adopt from Korea, but I knew God had a plan for us.

After much soul searching, and investigating different agencies as well, we chose Russia. When we agree to follow God he seems to enjoy taking us well out of our comfort zone. This time would be no different…I guessed I had better get used to flying!

Jeff and I met with the agency director who was a nice gentleman that seemed to really have a heart for kids. We filled out the necessary paperwork to begin the process. Each agency does things a little different.

At this particular one, it was explained to us that prospective parents are not given a data base of photos of children to choose from. Emotionally speaking, it would be hard to "choose" a child. Once we answered several questions regarding the child we might want our agency would then check their data bases of available children in the orphanages they worked with. They would email us one photo at a time, along with any health information they had. Sometimes a video might also be included. This was done so that prospective parents could review each child individually and not be overwhelmed in the process.

We often wondered, and asked many adopting parents, how would we know when we found the right child? Every person gave us the same answer, "When it's the right one, you'll just know."

The agency director told us that we should have a child in about ten months. We were on cloud nine as we walked out of the agency!

The next day…

Tragedy struck in Russia. Terrorists brought down two planes out of Moscow simultaneously. These extremists would turn out to be two female Chechen suicide bombers. It was then when we learned of the continuing war that had been going on for decades between Chechnya and Russia. The simultaneous plane crashes preceded more terrorist attacks in Russia. On August 31, 2004 a bomb killed 10 people in a Moscow subway station. Then, on September 1, 2004, began one of the most heinous attacks ever by insurgents, the Beslan hostage crisis. By the time it was over it would leave 335 people dead. Most of those who perished in that tragedy were children. I sat glued to the television trying to get news on the situation. I couldn't help but wonder if our future child was in that same area. My heart broke for what those people were going through. I noticed I was beginning to develop a sense of kinship with the people of Russia.

Another thought crossed my mind…what if we were sent to the area near Chechnya? I quickly dismissed the notion, telling myself the odds of us being in this region were slim due to the fact that Russia is a large country. Besides, I didn't think our agency would send us anywhere dangerous.

A couple of months later, I had been thinking, since our children from our previous marriages were older, and it was only my son who was still living at home, maybe we should consider adopting two children. It didn't seem fair to adopt just one, who might at times get lonely. We thought it would also be good if there were two so they would have a common bond with someone else in regards to their unique situation. Another issue was the language barrier, which would make a single adopted child feel even more isolated in a new home. These questions really made us think. Some children do well growing up alone and like it that way. God seemed to be leading us in a different direction. We contacted our agency and put in our request to adopt not one, but two children from Russia. The search was on!

Four

Mountain Of Documents

First we would need to complete a home study. When we received the checklist for the documents needed, there were sixteen items to complete. I thought we could easily accomplish this.

Just some of the documents needed…an application to adopt, Immigration, Naturalization Forms, INS forms, fingerprints, birth certificates, marriage certificates, divorce decrees, letters from friends, physician letters, bank letters, investment letters, tax returns, employment letters, CPA letters, letters from health insurance companies verifying health insurance, pediatrician letters, adoption decree, health records for biological children, and last but not least, a check for fees. *Whew!!!* Okay, maybe not as easy as we thought it would be, but these things were definitely do-able, they would just take some time.

What we didn't know then, was that this was just the beginning of a seemingly endless trail of paperwork. These first items were needed just to complete the home study. We would then need to complete state and federal level documents. Russia would also require its own set of paperwork. Not only would Russia require more documents, but we found out as time went on a lot of these documents expired quickly. Meaning, every three months we were being re-evaluated and checked by physicians, the FBI, national, and local police departments just to make sure we had not acquired any recent health issues or been recently arrested.

Once the home study was completed, and these documents completed, we breathed a sigh of relief, thinking the worst of the paperwork process was over. We were wrong! Next was the dossier. We would be completing two of these and hand carrying them to Russia. There were thirty-two items on the checklist for the dossier. After this, came a whole list of region specific documents which needed to be filled out. I'm glad we didn't know then what we know now. And I'm thankful God doesn't reveal the future to us.

We plowed through the paperwork as if it were an enormous mountain to be climbed in order to reach the prize. The prize was priceless, two small lives in need of a loving family to take care of them for a lifetime, and two parents in need of more children to love. Climbing the mountain was worth it.

Throughout the process we clung tightly to God and His promises. Although we knew in our hearts this is what He wanted us to do, and it was what we wanted too, there were times when it was extremely hard. Jeff and I fought a lot due to the stress and the finances it would take to fulfill our dream.

As far as the average American goes, I guess you would consider us middle class. But in our house, it certainly didn't feel that way. We, like most people lived paycheck to paycheck, with little left over each month. Where in the world would we ever get the money to adopt? I know it sounds crazy not to have thought this through. But in my experience, I have learned when God calls you to do something it's your job to act, and He will provide a way.

I had heard that sometimes major companies in the United States will provide adoption grants for people. This was in the days before "Go Fund Me" existed. I used the internet to search for such companies, and then started the letter writing process in order to apply for these grants. This was difficult and humbling for us. We were not in the habit of asking anyone for a handout, even if it was for a good cause.

I decided to start with 50 letters to various companies. Soon after receiving several rejection letters, most of them with some nasty remarks directed at us regarding asking for a handout, I gave up. I was surprised with the unprofessionalism at some of these corporations. In one of the letters, the person who responded to my request resorted to making fun of us. They wrote nasty comments on our denial letter then used liquid paper to cover it up. When I held the letter to the light I could see what they had written. It hurt.

There were many times when we became discouraged and wondered if maybe we weren't supposed to adopt. It was hard, and at times we were filled with doubt. But then the doubt spilled away and we felt strongly that this was something we were supposed to do. We wanted it more than ever. So we moved forward in faith with the help and prayers of our church, family, and friends.

While pouring over some of the many fund-raising ideas people had given us, we came to the conclusion that none of them would even come close to raising enough money to adopt. Maybe it was a lack of faith on our part. We had been shot down so many times by the rejection letters we didn't want to ask anyone for anything. Our only option was to mortgage our home. We had a decent amount of equity. We applied for a second mortgage and were approved. We then had the finances to move forward.

The endless trail of documents needed, kept us busy for the next several months. It was as though we had the "proverbial carrot" dangling from a stick in front of us the whole time, yet never quite reaching it.

We had set our sights on the agency's timeline of ten months. By the time we reached this point we should have been at the halfway mark. Looking back, we should have realized this was an unrealistic goal. Each case is different. Some take months, some take years. The best advice I can give anyone who is going through an adoption, is that they have got to learn to roll with the punches. And know that any and all things can go wrong.

Throughout the process our case was stalled many times. One of the reasons was because the Russian government was unsure if they were going to continue to allow Americans to adopt Russian children. There had been some cases of abuse by Americans involving adopted Russian children. I couldn't say I blamed them, after learning that a few of their adopted children, who had come to America, had died from abuse.

Also during this time, some glitches with our paperwork came up. One of the documents we had turned in had been stalled in the system for months. We were hoping it would get resolved. When it didn't, someone suggested we call our congressman, who at the time was Duncan Hunter Sr. He was extremely helpful and was able to get some answers regarding the clearance of this document. We learned our paperwork had been sitting on someone's desk in one department for months because they had a question about something on the document and couldn't get the other government agency to answer them. Duncan Hunter's office got the answer needed for the two parties and had it cleared up in a few days. I wish we would have known to call him much earlier on.

During the day while Jeff was at work, I would normally enjoy the quietness of our home. Now it was deafening and I hated it.

At least at home I was safe from the constant barrage of questions by genuinely concerned friends and family, who kept asking if we had heard any news yet. Each time we ran into someone we knew, I dreaded the inevitable question that would immediately follow their greeting, "Have you heard anything yet?" We had purposely waited several months to tell people about our plans to adopt until we were pretty sure it was going to happen. We had no idea of the delays that would take place and wished we would have waited longer to tell every one of our plans.

One particular December morning, I was having an emotionally tough time with the setbacks and waiting for news that seemingly would never come. Being in the quietness of our home on my days off was hard. The nursery had been finished for months. It was a constant reminder of the emptiness I felt. Some days I simply closed the door so as to not be reminded of the emptiness.

It had been almost a year since Jeff and I filed for the adoption of two children. The house was quiet…too quiet. I was in tears as I settled on the couch to pray.

As I poured out my heart to God I thought about a mother somewhere in Russia who was pregnant with the child she was about to give up. Was she scared? Does she know what she is about to do? What was she like? I prayed for her. I knew she was about to make the ultimate sacrifice and give us one of the most precious gifts we would ever receive.

While sitting there, I asked God for a sign. A word, or something to hold onto. I wanted to know that He was there and was in control.

I picked up my Bible and thumbed through the pages randomly. I stopped in the book of Luke. As I read, a scripture caught my attention, Luke 1:45, *"Blessed is she who has believed that what the Lord has said will be accomplished."* That's it! I knew instantly this would be the scripture I would hold onto to get me through. I wrote down the date next to the verse in my bible. It was December 1, 2004.

Five

Jeff and the Brake Guy

The New Year was upon us. As I walked around the house, I thought about how unfair it was to have this home all to ourselves. It wasn't a big house, but it definitely had room for two more. We wanted to share it and share what we had.

The baby's room was by far the prettiest room in the house. It had an incredible view of the mountains to the north. There were two cribs, which were able to convert to toddler beds in the event the children we adopted were older. A musical mobile hung in one of the cribs, in case one of the children was an infant. There were little hangers hanging in the closet and a white dresser to match the cribs. I would often come in this room to sit and dream about the day when it would be filled with laughter.

One day I went into the children's room. As I looked out the window, I noticed a rainbow in the sky. We live in an area that is considered a desert.

We don't get much rain, and certainly don't see rainbows very often. As I stared in awe at the bow in the sky, it gave me the sense of peace that I needed. It reminded me that God is in control. I knew things were going to work out the way they should.

We continued to plow through our daily lives with this huge thing hovering over us that was exciting, yet agonizing.

Guys always seem to have a different outlook on situations than women do. Jeff was definitely handling things much different than I was. When he wasn't getting discouraged, he was the exact opposite. He would tell everyone and anyone who would listen, about our decision to adopt. It would drive me crazy. I am the type of person who doesn't like to share things unless they've come to fruition.

Standing in line at Costco, Jeff would just blurt out to the person behind us our plans to adopt. They would usually look at us and say "congratulations." They were probably wondering why this total stranger felt the need to share this information with them. But, anyone who knows my husband knows he knows no strangers. Jeff shares his emotions with almost anyone he comes in contact with. It is a trait I admire in him, yet also makes me crazy.

Meanwhile, I was much more discreet about sharing our personal information. I had learned the hard way to stay quiet. For some reason, some women, feel the need to tell other women exactly what they think, whether it is hurtful or not. Most women I knew were happy for our decision to adopt and filled me with encouragement. Others felt the need to tell me what they thought was best. One woman said to me, "You know, all the love in the world can't "fix" these kids." I replied, "Well good thing my goal isn't to fix them, just love them and give them a good home." Another woman was upset because we were bringing more "foreigners" to this country. I was taken aback. Sadly, the negative comments we receive in life sometimes are the ones we remember the most. Thankfully, not everyone felt that way. In fact, almost everyone else we encountered supported us and our decision.

One day while I was working my cell phone rang. It was Jeff's number. I didn't pick it up right away. He called back a second time immediately after the first. Thinking something was really important, I picked up. Jeff was anxiously waiting on the other end. "Guess what?!" he said. "What?" I replied. "We got the brakes done on the car for free!" At which point, I was a little irritated because the news could have waited. But now I was curious. "Why did we get the brakes done for free?" I asked. "You know how you are always telling me not to tell everyone that we are adopting?" "Well this time I was talking to the guy who was doing our brakes about our plans. The guy was so touched by our story that he decided to do the brakes for free!"

It was one of so many kind and generous things that our friends, clients, family, and strangers, did for us during the course of the whole process. This time Jeff was right about sharing our story. It really helped us out. Getting the brakes done for free was especially huge. What most people didn't realize at the time was how broke we were. Because the process was taking much longer than anticipated, it had cost us thousands more than we had originally estimated. Things were already tight, and now they were worse. Things started to get intense between us and we fought a lot. The pressure of the adoption was similar to what some of my friends had gone through during their infertility treatments.

Six

Heartbreak

It was now October, a little over a year since we filled out our application to adopt. There was still no word on when two children would be available. A hard fact to accept when there are close to 700,000 orphans in Russia. Stress had been taking a hard toll on us. Jeff, who was usually a happy-go-lucky kind of guy, was more tired than usual and had gotten temperamental. He was moody a lot of the time, and so was I.

The stress manifested itself in me on a physical level. I started getting sick a lot. There were other physical changes in my body as well. I made an appointment with my doctor to find out if there was anything, other than stress, going on.

During the appointment with my doctor, I fully expected to be told that my problems were normal due to the pressure I was under. Only, that wasn't the case. She informed me that I had started pre-menopause. *Are you serious?!* I thought menopause was something that happened later in someone's life. I was surprised.

There was more…during the exam she had found a cyst on my ovary along with several fibroid tumors. These types of tumors are usually common, and not necessarily cancerous. Ovarian cysts can even go away on their own. But for us, the news was devastating. Until it was determined the cyst was benign, it would mean I could not pass the physical for the adoption, bringing the whole thing to a screeching halt. I felt like I had just been kicked in the stomach. I waited until I got to the car before I would allow the flood of tears.

Within a few days of this news we received another blow…there had been word from our agency about two children who would possibly be coming up for adoption soon. We were hopeful but told no one for fear of another setback. Then, in the middle of my sorrow over the doctor's diagnosis, our agency called to let us know the children had been adopted by a Russian family. Their citizens get first rights at adopting their children before foreigners.

I felt so out of control. I was upset, angry, and confused. I cried a lot that week. We started to wonder if we had heard God wrong when we made the decision to adopt.

The Sunday after we received the bad news from the doctor, Jeff and I were in church listening to a message our pastor was giving. The title of the sermon was, "Building a Great Heart-Staying on Course in the Ups and Downs." One of the many things made clear to us during the sermon, was that "downs" in your life do not mean you've done something wrong, or made the wrong decision. Sometimes when you do something big that you truly believe God has led you to do; things get hard and may not go according to planned. It doesn't mean you made the wrong choice.

There are a lot of stories in the Bible of men who were led directly by God himself to do huge things. Many of them… Moses, Joseph, and King David, all had major setbacks and also questioned if they were doing the right thing. I had to remind myself of this many times, and took comfort in reading about their struggles. Moses, Joseph, and David were faithful in following the Lord, and in return He did great things in their lives.

The days passed slowly while waiting for the results of the tests my doctor ran. Our home seemed emptier than ever, but I kept holding on to God's promise in the scripture I had found last December. I recited it in my head constantly…*"Blessed is she who believes what the Lord has said will come to pass."*

Through it all we kept praying and asking for prayer. Thankfully we had a great home group we belonged to through our church. I don't know what we would have done without them. They prayed for us, listened, cried with us, and never gave up hope. We leaned on them constantly.

Another month had gone by while waiting to see if the ovarian cyst would dissolve on its own or if it was something more serious. *Would our dream be crushed after we had come so far?* And what if it was cancer? I could hardly think anymore. We had definitely hit one of our lowest points.

The waiting was grueling and tensions were high. I held on to the fact that when the timing is right God will not abandon us. He makes no mistakes.

Finally, when it was time for my second visit, my doctor gave me the good news. The cyst was gone! It had dissolved on its own which meant it was not cancerous. The fibroid tumors were still there, but at least they were benign. A huge wave of relief washed over me. It was another mountain climbed and conquered. I was able to get the health clearance we needed to move forward.

Seven

Thanksgiving

It was one week before Thanksgiving when we received a call from the adoption agency telling us to open the e-mail they sent us. The director had forwarded a picture and a profile of a baby girl who would possibly be available for adoption in a couple of weeks. That is, if a Russian family didn't adopt her before her first birthday. Jeff and I nearly trampled each other trying to get to our computer to open up the e-mail. This was the first photo we had ever received from the agency.

In an instant, so many questions flashed through my mind. *What does she look like? How old is she? What is her story? Where is she right now?*

Our computer was old and slow, but on that day, it was slower than ever. Once the email was opened it seemed to take forever for the picture to load. We both stood there, wide eyed, anxiously staring at the screen. The room was silent as the picture slowly emerged.

A tiny, almost bald baby, with big eyes appeared. She was wrapped up like a burrito. We could only see her head. She looked scared, and she probably was.

According to her profile she wasn't quite a year old, but to us she appeared much younger. Jeff and I were in awe at this little creation. It was love at first sight. Her name was Anya. There was no question, we wanted this baby!

We called our agency director to let him know we were definitely interested. There was only one huge problem…would another child come up for adoption before this one was adopted by someone else? We were trying to bring home two children at the same time. It wasn't possible for us to travel to Russia more than the two times, as was required by their government. The first trip was to meet your child, the second was to bring the child home. All we could do was wait.

Thanksgiving morning…Jeff and I woke up early to drive to my parent's house, which was about two hours away. While we were packing the phone rang. It was my mom. She said she was sorry, but we had better not come up. My dad had the flu and she didn't want us to catch it. Thanksgiving dinner would have to wait until the weekend. Maybe he would be better by then. Knowing my parents, my dad had to have been pretty sick to call off Thanksgiving.

A little while later my mom called again. She said my dad was getting worse and she was taking him to the hospital. Naturally, my first instinct was to drive up there, but she didn't want us to drive all that way if it wasn't serious. "Besides," she said. "What good would it do for all of us to be sitting around in the emergency room for hours when it was probably the flu." My mom is a strong woman who can handle just about anything. We decided to stay home and wait for her to call and let us know what was happening.

Jeff and I tinkered around the house that day, trying to keep busy. It was several hours later when my mom finally called us back to let us know he did not have the flu. It was his appendix that was causing the symptoms. It had burst, and he was going into the operating room for surgery. Mom told us again there was no need to come up. "There really isn't anything you can do." She said. "He will probably be home in a day or so and you can come up then." We agreed. The turkey she had thawed never got cooked.

On Sunday morning, while coming out of church, I switched on my cell phone. I was surprised to see I had a message from my mom to call her. It was unusual for my parents to leave messages. I knew something was wrong. I called her right away. She said my dad was having trouble breathing and the doctors had discovered not one, but several pulmonary embolisms. It was serious and I needed to get up there. I kicked myself for not driving up there two days ago even though she told me not to. I packed and left immediately for the hospital. I made the trip alone because we had no idea how long I would be gone. Jeff couldn't use any of his days off from work. We needed all of them for the trip to Russia. If, we ever got that second phone call.

During the two hour drive, it was the first time I had not been thinking about the adoption. For so many months it had occupied pretty much my every waking thought.

Over the next several days, my mom, some close family friends, and me, kept an almost constant vigil next to my dad's hospital bed in ICU. He was a strong man who could do almost anything, except fight this thing going on in his body. Seeing him like this was really hard on all of us. It was the first time I could ever remember my dad being sick. The days dragged on, but I was thankful to be there with my parents.

After about a week in ICU, his health had finally improved. The blood clots had dissipated, and he was no longer in danger. He could possibly go home in a day or two. Thank you God!

I decided to take a walk to get some fresh air. I also desperately needed some caffeine. While walking to the hospital cafeteria I thought about how lucky we were to have my dad still there with us, and about the timing of everything. *What if this had happened while we were in Russia?* God is always around and always works things out, I told myself.

While making my way back through the long corridor, coffee in hand, thoughts of Jeff, work, and home were swirling through my head. The ringing of my cell phone pulled me out of my trance. The caller ID showed it was Jeff. I answered, and received the shock of my life…he was calling to tell me our agency had located a second little girl ready for adoption. And…Anya was still available!

The agency asked us, if we were willing to go forward with the adoption, then could we be on a plane to Russia in a week?! *A week?! Wow!!!* I stood there in the hallway stunned, no longer needing the caffeine I was holding in my other hand.

I hung up the phone and went to my dad's room to give my parents the good news. They were really excited, but also in a bit of shock. I think we were all thinking…*Wow! This is really happening!*

I needed to get home. Within a few hours, I was packed and headed back to San Diego. I couldn't wait to see the picture our agency had sent us. Jeff had already printed it out so I didn't have to wait on our dinosaur of a computer to see her. Again, this was before smart phones came out.

I could hardly believe my eyes. She was this sweet tiny thing. She was bundled up in a white fluffy blanket with a matching hat. She looked as though she had just come out of the cold Siberian tundra. Her name was Svetlana, and she had also recently turned one year old. Once again we were in love with this little human we had never met. *Hmmm…looks like we might be raising "twins!"*

"Blessed is she who has believed that what the Lord has said will be accomplished." It didn't hit me right then. It wasn't even until a few months later, when I was going through the pages of my bible. I ran across the scripture God had led me to on that cold December morning one year ago. The date I had written in the margin of my bible was December 1, 2004. I realized it was on that day that Anya was born. To think, in all of my despair, that day in particular, God had not only heard my prayer, but was answering it as well. In my grief, while crying out to him for something to hold on to, she was coming into this world!

Eight

Time to Go!

The agency wasted no time in moving us forward. How could it be that after all this time of planning and preparing, we still had what seemed like a million things to do to get ready to go?! After waiting for over a year and a half, we now had only six days to get things in order so we could leave!

Jeff had let his employers know months ago about the adoption and that he may have to take time off with very little notice. They had already approved his leave of absence. I was self-employed so it was a little more challenging but it worked out. For the most part, my clients were supportive.

Jeff and I were filled with a renewed sense of energy. Our home, which lately had become a place of despair and discouragement, was filled with an excited chaos as we rushed to make the last minute preparations to leave the country.

For the last several months the bedroom we had finished for the girls had since become our staging area for the trip. During that time our luggage had been laying open on the floor in their room. Whenever we thought of something we might need to bring with us we would toss it in one of the suitcases. Every so often the items were changed out and replaced, depending on what season it was. At one point we packed sunscreen and mosquito repellant. Now, those items were no longer needed because it was winter. It also happened to be the coldest winter on record in Russia. *It figures! I hate the cold.*

With that in mind, I drove to the local sporting goods store and picked up at least a dozen packets of boot and hand warmers. They are small chemical filled packets that when shaken give off heat for several hours. You can then place them in your gloves and boots to keep warm. Thankfully I had already found a down coat, which was no easy task, considering the fact that we lived in San Diego, and no one I know has ever needed a down coat while living here.

Now if we just could get our visas in time for our departure, we would be ready to go. Russia required a visa in order to enter their country. Visas expire in a short amount of time, so it is not something you want to get until it's close to your departure date. Our application had been filled out months ago which would help speed along the process. Meanwhile our agency worked fast to finalize the details of the flights, tickets, hotels, drivers, interpreters, coordinator, and everything else that needed to be done on their end. The days were now flying by!

Sometime after dark, on the night before we were ready to leave, there was a knock at the door. Our Visas had arrived. *That was cutting it close!*

That night, with our bags packed and the house in order, Jeff and I realized how hungry we were. There really wasn't anything to eat in the house that was easy, and we had already cleaned out the fridge. We drove down to the local Chinese restaurant and picked up some food to take home.

While we ate we chatted excitedly about our upcoming adventure. We were changing the course of history in our lives forever. I envisioned toddlers running around our house playing and laughing. We were so excited to finally meet our girls and wondered what it would be like to actually hold them.

When dinner was over we tore the wrapper off of our fortune cookies. Jeff broke his in half to retrieve the fortune inside. "You're not going to believe what mine says!" He exclaimed. He passed it over to me so I could read it. I stared at the fortune in disbelief… The fortune read, *"You will visit some faraway land that has long been in your waking thoughts."* Chills ran up and down my spine. I laughed out loud in amazement. It was almost as if God was winking at us. I don't know what God looks like. In my mind, I envisioned this kind and loving image of an older Jesus, smiling and laughing with us as a father would when he loves his children deeply.

Nine

Los Angeles to Moscow

Sleep did not come easy. We were much too excited. The big day was finally here! It was just after midnight when we got out of bed to get ready to make the two-hour drive to the Los Angeles Airport. We had an 8:00 AM flight. As we loaded our luggage into the car in the middle of the night, it felt as though we were embarking on some grand adventure. The streets were dark and quiet. There was a light drizzle coming out of the fog making everything seem surreal.

Interstate five which was normally grid-locked seemed a dark and desolate highway at this hour, something I had never seen before.

We stored our car at a lot in Los Angeles then took a shuttle to the airport. We were now completely in the hands of others, who unknowingly, were the first of many who would be helping us fulfill our dream.

Once we boarded the plane and were seated for the first of our three flights, I realized it was the first time in over a year when Jeff and I could finally sit back and relax. For now, there were no more forms to fill out, no more errands to run, and nothing to do except enjoy the ride. I plugged in my earbuds and scrolled through the various radio stations. I stopped on a selection playing Christmas music. As I listened to the songs of the season I smiled. God's timing is amazing. Not only was it almost Christmas, we would be meeting one, or both of the girls, on my birthday. It was almost unbelievable that this was actually happening!

During the flight we passed the time doing a lot of crossword puzzles. This was just before the variety of electronic devices that would soon be coming out. The skies were clear and the sun was now shining brightly over the snow-covered Rocky Mountains. The sight was breathtaking.

About mid-way into the flight, I turned on the screen on the back of the seat in front of me to see what movies were playing. One of my favorite movies was on, "The Goonies." I had even visited the town of Astoria a few years back to see where it was filmed. *God was winking again.*

We landed in New York City at JFK. We would have a long layover until our flight to Moscow.

While waiting in the airport we met with a few other couples who were on our next flight, and also adopting children from Russia. I remember one woman who was traveling alone. She was a single parent who was adopting a child by herself. I remember thinking how brave she was for going through all of this alone. I wished I had that kind of courage.

Jeff and I stared out the windows of the airport. The sun was setting and it had snowed. The clouds in the sky were beautifully swirled in pink, reds and blues. Off in the distance we could see the Manhattan skyline. There was lightning over the city. Each event, no matter how minor to the rest of the world, was like a gift from God. If we look and listen, we can see that He grants us these little pleasures in life so we can know we matter to Him.

It was time to board our next airplane. It was a Russian carrier that would be taking us from New York to Moscow. As we boarded, I was feeling pretty excited and very nervous. Upon entering the plane it felt like we were in another world. The crew and almost all 300 passengers were Russian. We were greeted in their language by the flight attendants.

I had thought, since we were on an international flight, we might get to watch a couple of movies. There were only two over-head monitors on the plane. As we flew, the display on the screens showed a map of our projected path using a tiny blip symbolizing our current location. It showed our location along with the altitude and outside temperature. We were at 40,000 feet and it was -65 degrees outside.

I took in the sounds of people quietly chatting in their native language. I wanted to capture every moment in time.

In the year before we traveled I read several books on Russia. I wanted to learn about its people, their culture, and their history. One of the books I read was about what *not* to do while visiting their country. The Russian people have a lot of superstitions and cultural etiquette that are different from Americans. I learned that seemingly innocent things we do here in America could be mistaken as rude and sometimes illegal in their country. For example, if you were to smile at someone you didn't know on the street in Russia, they might be wondering what you were up to or possibly consider you as arrogant, as opposed to Americans, who smile to show kindness. It's not that the Russian people aren't kind, they simply see smiling at strangers as unnecessary.

It is also considered taboo to shake hands across a door-way. They believe it to be bad luck. Not bringing a gift when you visit someone's home is a huge social faux pas. We were warned about this one before we left. It was customary to bring gifts for everyone who helped us, including the orphanage directors. This custom stressed me out almost as much as everything else did. How in the world do you figure out what to buy total strangers in a foreign country, while at the same time not look like you are being cheap? Some friends of ours purchased gold bracelets for all of their people. There was no way we could afford those types of gifts. Thankfully we were told we wouldn't have to worry about gift-giving until the second trip. As I write this, I realized I never thought why it didn't offend anyone when we didn't bring gifts for the first trip.

Later in the flight we were treated to a large dinner and dessert. As we flew over the Atlantic we kept looking at the overhead monitor waiting for the map to disappear and a movie to start…it never happened. We sat there for 8 hours watching the little blip on the screen slowly move across the continents. Sometime, late in the evening, while staring at the screen above our heads, we were lulled to sleep.

Movie aside, I will say that this airline knew how to feed people. We woke up to the smells and sounds of breakfast. Another large meal was being served. The sun was up and the plane was bustling with activity as passengers were moving around the cabin.

After breakfast we were handed some forms to fill out. They were written in the Russian language. We had no idea what they said; we could only assume they were declaration forms for entering the country. The flight attendants were of no help. They spoke no English; at least that is what they conveyed to us. The gentleman sitting next to me noticed our struggle in trying to figure out what to do with the forms. He spoke English and was kind enough to help us fill out the necessary paperwork. Soon after this, we landed.

Ten

Passport Control-Soviet Style

I grew up in an era when the Americans and the Russians feared each other. The Soviet Union and the United States were the two super powers of the world. There was always tension between the countries, and the fear that at any moment either one could push "the button", to start a nuclear war. I don't think many people born after the 1980's grasp how intense things were. People in both countries were scared of the other.

At the time of our adoption it had only been about fifteen years since the Soviet regime had collapsed and tensions had eased a bit. Russia has a dark history of war, which includes conquering and being conquered, making their people have a tendency not to trust strangers. I wasn't sure how well Americans would be received and it made me uneasy.

When we disembarked the aircraft it felt like my stomach did a flip inside of me. We were far from home, crossing a border that made us feel vulnerable and so foreign. What if we needed help? It was just the two of us. In reality God was there too. He had brought us there. We would need to rely on our faith in Him to take care of us.

In the airport there were very few signs in English. Not having a clue as to where we were supposed to go we followed the other passengers who exited our plane. We made our way alongside the glass windows with a view of the snow covered tarmac outside. We walked through some corridors, and then finally down a flight of stairs into what appeared to be a basement.

As we descended the stairs, passengers made their way to one of the several lines being formed in front of the glass booths. There were several stern looking female officials standing guard. They appeared to be dressed in military uniforms, but I couldn't be sure.

We learned from other American passengers that this was passport control. I had read about passport control back home. And from what I read, it was *not* going to be a pleasant experience. This was where their officials scrutinized you, and your passport, in an intimidating stare down until you were about to crack, all the while, deciding whether or not to allow you entry into their country.

Passengers who had just arrived were standing at a counter filling out forms, and then heading to the lines that were being formed at the booths. We made our way to the counters, not really knowing what to do next.

The forms people were filling out were written entirely in the Russian language. There were none with an English translation on them. Thankfully, it was at that moment, when we ran into the man who was sitting next to us on the airplane. He was kind enough once again to help us fill out the paperwork, which we did, then headed for the lines.

At the beginning of each line there was a remotely activated metal bar which allowed a single person access to stand in front of the booth where the guards were positioned. Two guards shared a booth, making two lines. They stood with their backs to each other, each checking passports that came through their separate lines.

The guards stood behind a glass window with a small pass-through at the bottom to allow documents to be exchanged. There were mirrors up above and behind you. This made it so the officials could also see your back while they were questioning you. It was very intimidating. Thankfully, this was not the trip where we would have to bring the thousands of dollars in cash for the "donation" to the orphanage.

While waiting in line we befriended another American couple who were also adopting a child. This couple had also read the same things about passport control, and how intimidating it was. By the time it was our turn to go through, the other American woman and I had ourselves pretty worked up with worry.

It was now our turn. One person at a time was allowed. Jeff sent me ahead of him. As I made my way past the metal bar, it locked behind me. I was surprised to see that all of the officials in the booths were women.

I handed the female official my passport. The other American woman was on the other side also showing her passport to the official who shared a booth with the woman who was looking at mine.

The scrutinizing began. The female guard looked me up and down. She stared at my passport for a long time. I broke out in a sweat. Nothing was said, just staring and glaring. Finally, the guard who was inspecting my passport turned around to the guard behind her and began speaking to her in Russian. All kinds of scenarios were running through my head. *Was there a problem with my paperwork? Would they allow us into their country? Would I be searched?*

Then something completely unexpected happened…the two female guards began laughing. Both looked down at our passports trying to gain their composure.

As soon as they looked at me and the other American woman, they would start laughing again. It got to the point where they were actually laughing so hard tears were coming out of their eyes. I stood there somewhat relieved, but also feeling a bit humiliated. I quickly decided that a bit of being made fun of by Russian officials was much better than being interrogated. I stood there quietly until they were finished with their hysterics.

Jeff and the other American passed through the booth in the same manner, the officials laughing at them too. The guards probably saw the look of fear on our faces and knew we were amateurs at international travel. I could still see them snickering as we walked away. We will never know what was so funny about us that it made two stone faced guards laugh so hard they cried. I was just glad to have made it through the first checkpoint.

Our next line was Customs. Surprisingly, we went through quickly. Then made our way into the area where people were waiting for passengers to arrive. It was then when we finally saw something familiar to us, a large piece of cardboard with our last name written on it. It was being held up by a petite Russian woman who greeted us in English. I can't tell you how relieved we were to see that sign. To know we weren't alone, and that someone in the world knew where we were, and where we were supposed to be was reassuring.

The woman holding the sign introduced herself as Olga. She lived in Russia and worked for our adoption agency. She would be our interpreter while we were in Moscow. As she directed us out of the crowd of people she asked us how our flight went but didn't make much small talk. Once we cleared the crowd of people she picked up the pace through the airport, as Jeff and I hurriedly followed behind her.

My friends back home have always commented on how fast I walk wherever I go. My son jokes about it to his friends. Telling them, "In our family, if you don't walk as fast as my mom, you get left behind!" Jeff, on the other hand is usually about ten paces behind me. He enjoys taking in every moment. That being said, the pace at which I walk was nothing compared to Olga. Poor Jeff, she was walking so fast he could barely keep up. He was starting to lag. As we sped through the airport I kept a close eye on him, while also trying to keep up with Olga, and listen to her instructions regarding our itinerary. Because of the pace at which we were walking, I was under the impression that our next flight would be leaving soon. It turned out that wasn't the case. During our time in their country we learned that everyone walks fast, especially the women.

Eleven

When Not to Dress Like an Eskimo

Olga led us to the main lobby of the airport. She told us we would be waiting there for several hours until it was time to go to the other airport in Moscow to catch our second flight. We were confused as to why we couldn't just fly out of this one. I don't remember what her answer was regarding the two airports.

Once we were in the main area Olga said she would be back when it was time to take us to our next flight. "You're leaving?!" I said with a bit of shock. We had just met her, and yet I already felt she was abandoning us. I guess it made sense, why should she wait with us for hours when she had other things to do. I was tired and starting to feel vulnerable in a foreign place.

I often wish I could be a free spirit like Jeff. He is often happy, social, and goes with the flow on just about everything. He was perfectly fine being left in the airport. Olga pointed us in the direction of an American food chain. It was the only place to eat with menus in English. Then she left.

After eating we hauled all of our stuff to the place where Olga said she would meet us. We still had several hours to go until she came back. Jeff spread himself out on some seats and went right to sleep. I marvel, and yet am somewhat irritated by his ability to sleep wherever we go. It's an inside joke among many of our close friends who have often heard my rantings at him about it. He even fell asleep at the zoo once!

While Jeff slept I made my way to the restrooms to wash my face and brush my teeth. It had been over twenty four hours since we left our home. Even though my body was exhausted, my adrenalin was still pumping with excitement. As I gazed in the mirror at my bloodshot eyes, I could hardly believe we were actually there. I made my way back to the lobby and sat next to Jeff who was already snoring.

While I sat watching the other passengers, I came to the realization of how under-dressed we were. Naturally, since we were going to Russia in the winter, and traveling a long distance, we dressed accordingly. We both had worn comfortable and warm clothes. Jeff was wearing athletic pants, a wool sweater, and sheepskin boots. He had also brought along a big coat. I was wearing slacks, a wool sweater, and a down ski jacket with a fluffy hood, complete with snow boots. All of the travelers we saw were dressed impeccably. I could hear the click-clack of high heels as women walked back and forth through the airport. Looking down at my boots I felt embarrassed. No one was wearing them!

The women in Moscow wore beautiful wool, and sometimes fur coats. They all seemed to be wearing dresses and high heels. I wondered how they could walk in them through the snow. We were the only travelers looking like we were going to Alaska to live in an igloo. Maybe that's why the officials back in passport control were laughing at us. We really stood out. I made a mental note to wear different clothes for our second trip.

After much people watching, several crossword puzzles, and a few catnaps, Olga returned to the airport just like she said she would.to take us to our next flight.

The three of us made our way to the main exit of the airport. It was dark by now. The opening of the doors sent a blast of bitter cold right through me. It was four degrees outside.

We made our way through the slush and snow to the car where our driver was waiting. I wondered how Olga's feet were keeping warm, and was now thankful for my snow boots, no matter how stupid they looked.

We were introduced to our driver, Alex. He was standing near a tiny little car. I could not for the life of me figure out how the four of us and our luggage were going to fit. Jeff and I each had one large suitcase, a medium size one, and a carry on. That made six pieces of luggage and four people. I thought they would have to call the agency here in Moscow to get us a bigger car.

Alex placed our luggage into his car while Jeff and I got into the back seat. Watching him load the car was like watching a live game of Tetris where you have to fit all of the different sizes of blocks together. While he crammed everything into the hatchback I wondered if he was secretly cursing us for the amount of luggage we brought with us. I also wondered if they had ever had an adoption visit in which Americans brought so many suitcases that they weren't able to fit in the car.

I searched behind me for a seatbelt only to discover that there were none. It would turn out that none of the cars we were in during our stay had rear seatbelts.

Alex finished loading the car, and we were on our way. He somehow managed to make it all fit. As we drove through the snow-covered streets of Moscow the city was bustling with activity. Alex cut in and out of traffic. There were no definitive lanes, just mass amounts of cars zipping through the streets, many times coming dangerously close to one another. It reminded me of driving in Tijuana.

Olga informed us that she would not be traveling with us to the southern region of Russia, but another adoption coordinator would be making the trip. Our next stop before the airport would be to pick her up. I wondered to myself, *how were we going to fit one more person into this car?!*

We turned down a small side street and pulled over in front of an apartment building. Out came a strikingly beautiful woman with long dark hair. She was wearing a dark skirt, high heeled boots, a red scarf, and was wrapped in a black shawl. She was carrying a small suitcase.

Alex got out and worked some magic in the trunk of the car. Somehow he managed to fit all of the bags in and still close the lid of the hatchback. Olga introduced us to the woman. Her name was Nadia. She would be our Adoption Coordinator for the southern region. It didn't appear that she spoke English. *This should be interesting,* I thought. *How was she going to be our adoption coordinator if she didn't speak any English?*

Soon we were on our way again. The car ride reminded me of Mr. Toad's Wild Ride at Disneyland. Nadia and Olga chatted away in Russian while Jeff and I sat squished and clueless while taking in the sights of

Moscow.

It wasn't long before nature called...the bumpy car ride made my bladder feel as though it was going to burst. I waited as long as I could before I said something. *God knows, I didn't want to be the person who made us have to find a restroom.* I finally spoke up. I asked if there was somewhere where we could stop. Olga mentioned a McDonald's where we could go.

We pulled into the driveway of the fast food chain. I peeled myself out of the car praying I could get back in again.

Inside, the restaurant looked similar and yet so foreign at the same time. On my way to find the restrooms I glanced overhead at the menu. I couldn't read the writing. It was written in Russian. It was so bizarre. Here was something so familiar to me, yet I couldn't read the menu.

Olga directed me through the crowd and up the stairs. It was like being in a night club packed with people. On the door of the restroom there was a sign I couldn't read. Olga said it was out of order. We would have to find another bathroom. Now I really had to go! Quickly we made our way back downstairs and out of the building. She said that there were some other restrooms not far from where we were.

We made our way across the parking lot, through the snow, and down the street. There were some portable toilets sitting in about two feet of snow off to the side of a building. Sitting beside them, was an old woman in a chair. She was holding a container for money. I gathered she was the attendant. I felt bad for her. Here was this old woman sitting on a chair in the snow at night monitoring the public restrooms. She must have been freezing.

I had no Rubles on me. We hadn't exchanged our money yet. I swallowed hard and asked Olga if I could borrow some change. This was somewhat humiliating and humbling. I had just met these people and now I had to borrow money to go to the bathroom. She politely obliged.

Back on the road, on our drive through Moscow, we learned that Nadia did in fact speak English. She just didn't care to because it was difficult for her. This was a relief. After all, she was going to be the person we depended on for the duration of our trip.

Thirteen

Scariest Plane Ride Ever

At the airport a shuttle picked us up from the terminal to take us to the awaiting aircraft. It was late in the evening and snow was falling. There were no weather tunnels to walk through. Nadia, Jeff, and myself traipsed across the snow covered asphalt towards the airplane which was covered in snow. The stairs to the aircraft were decorated with brightly colored Christmas lights. It was a nice touch considering the time of year.

Jeff had the camera out, and as we approached he snapped a picture. Just then, and out of nowhere, came two Russian officials running towards us. They were speaking firmly to us in Russian while waving frantically at our camera. Nadia informed us that taking pictures was forbidden. We apologized in English and put the camera away. I'm not sure if they knew how sorry we were, but they must have understood because they walked away and left us alone. We were there barely a day and had already committed a crime.

When we boarded I was surprised to see how old the aircraft was. It appeared to be right out of the 1950's. Being absolutely terrified to fly, I thought my chances of survival would be best if I didn't board. My first instinct was to turn around and go back down the stairs, but there were throngs of people behind me making an escape difficult. I sucked in hard and got on the plane.

Nadia found her seat in one of the first rows on the right side. Our seats were on the other side and further back. I was a bit disappointed we wouldn't be sitting next to her. I was hoping she could interpret the announcements to us.

I walked down the center aisle of the aircraft and located my seat. Something was not quite right. My seat appeared to be broken. The back portion was laying all the way forward resting on the bottom. With my palms already sweating, I picked up the back portion of the seat and returned it to the upright position. The top part went flying back making a lot of noise as it bounced into its correct position. Jeff said we were on a cargo plane which also carried passengers. The seats were designed that way on purpose. That information did *not* make me feel better!

I placed some of my things on the overhead shelf above our seats where compartments would normally be. I hoped we didn't have any turbulence or else the bags stored there would come flying out. Maybe I would get knocked out by something, and then I wouldn't have to worry so much about everything because I would be unconscious for the rest of the flight.

As soon as I sat down the metal lunch tray in front of me bounced outward and hit my knees hard. I tried to put it back in its proper upright position only to have it fall again and hit my lap. It was broken and would have to stay down for the duration of the flight.

Once seated, I noticed my bottom just kept sinking until it was lodged into the frame of the seat. There was no seat bottom, just a worn out cushion. I most likely would not be getting out of my seat without the use of a crowbar. I searched for the seatbelt only to find that it too was also broken.

I ransacked my purse looking for my bottle of Dramamine, or something of the like. I found the bottle wishing I had brought Xanax instead. I quickly took one, placing it under my tongue to make it work faster; not being sure if that would even work.

The knees of the person behind me were pressed up against my back. Most of the cushion in the back of the seat was gone too. I then noticed that my knees were also pressing into the person's back who was sitting in front of me. That passenger didn't seem to mind. As a matter of fact, everyone else was settling in quite nicely. I seemed to be the only one who had issues with anything.

While we waited for take-off, I carefully studied my surroundings. I checked for locations of exits in case of an emergency. At the front of the center aisle, located on the wall directly in front of the bulkhead seat, was one of those laminated placards you usually see in the seat pocket in front of you. They have the location of the emergency exits printed on them. This card was crookedly scotch-taped onto the wall in front of the first seat. It was the only one on the entire airplane. I couldn't see far enough to read where the exits were, but came to the conclusion it probably didn't matter much. If there was some sort of crash, judging by the way I was lodged into the seat, I wouldn't be able to get out anyway!

On the window I moved the curtain aside…yes, I said curtain. The window was covered in snow. We couldn't see anything. The flight attendants were busy carrying on with their normal duties. Jeff was quietly observing the things going on around him. Inside he was probably secretly dreading having to deal with my hysterics during take-off and landing.

The plane shook as the engines roared to life. I was a wreck. My stomach was twisted in knots. The window was still covered with snow making it impossible to get one last look at solid ground. I was gripping the armrests as tight as I could. The aircraft was vibrating unusually hard. This wasn't a noise or feel I was accustomed to on previous flights. Jeff shot me a glance that told me he too was concerned.

We were straining to get a glimpse of the outside, when all of the sudden the snow blew off of the window. Alongside of us on the tarmac was a big flatbed truck. Sitting on the bed of the truck was what appeared to be an old jet engine. It was on some sort of platform which was rotating back and forth. It wasn't the engine on our airplane that roared to life, it was the engine on the platform. It was blowing an incredible blast of wind towards us. There was a man sitting behind it guiding it back and forth with controls. The blast of air was blowing the snow off of our plane. Other passengers didn't even flinch. It was then when I realized how incredibly efficient the Russians are. *Why throw away a perfectly good airplane engine when you can reuse it as a snow blower?*

We had not yet taken off when the flight attendants were heading down the aisle pushing a silver cart. It had drinks on it, mostly alcoholic beverages. *What a great idea! Why wait until we were in the air to have a drink?*

After drinks were served and cups collected, attendants came around offering hard candies to each passenger. It wasn't long before everyone was asleep even though we hadn't even left the ground.

We had been sitting on the tarmac for close to an hour when the silence was shattered by the obnoxious ringing of a bell. It sounded like one you would hear on a really old telephone. The flight attendants hurriedly put away the drink carts. I swore I could smell someone smoking...they probably were. Things we get offended by at home didn't seem to matter much in other places of the world. I had quit smoking several years ago, but if there was ever a time I had wanted a cigarette, now was one of those times! The engines roared to life. This time they were in fact the engines attached to our airplane. It was still snowing.

That Sunday night in Russia was Sunday morning back home of the same day. At that exact moment, on the other side of the planet, the church we normally attended was alive and full of people. The worship band was no doubt playing their hearts out while the congregation sang praises to God. Sitting there, in my mind, I transported myself back home to my church. I imagined myself sitting with my friends and singing to God. I prayed we would make it safely off the ground.

We taxied down the runway in the dark snowy night. I squeezed Jeff's hand until it was white from lack of circulation. He was used to the pain by now.

The aircraft lifted off the ground, but seemed to be struggling. I could hear the whine of the engines. They were working hard to gain altitude. I wondered if there was ice on the wings, or if the snow was more than it could handle. I tried to remind myself that this was Russia, they flew all the time in the snow and they knew how to do it.

The high-pitched noise of the engines made it sound as though they were in top gear. Then the pitch changed to something much lower, almost a bogging down noise. This back and forth sound from the engines continued as we slowly, and I mean slowly, gained altitude. This continued for what seemed like forever. We then banked hard left. My emotions got the best of me. I started laughing and crying at the same time. It was a hard ugly cry mixed in with some laughter. I was terrified we wouldn't make it, but at the same time laughing at the ridiculous situation I was in, considering that I am so afraid to fly.

I also desperately wanted to meet the girls. This last year had been an emotionally charged process. It often felt like a roller coaster ride. I also had not slept since we left San Diego on Friday morning. That was two days ago.

I praised God for every foot of altitude we gained. As we climbed higher, my grip on Jeff's hand slightly softened. He is so patient with me sometimes. We looked in each other's eyes. He was sympathetic to my fears, but what he was really thinking, was how much fun he was having. One of Jeff's great qualities is that he has fun no matter what the situation is. I shook my head in annoyance. I was irritated at what a great time he was having in the midst of my sheer terror, and our possible demise. The aircraft finally leveled off as it carried us on our journey south.

Thirteen

Diverted Flight

About mid-flight we were served dinner. Jeff and I were famished. On the tray in front of us were a variety of foods. The first one to catch my attention was the sardine. Jeff said it was herring. I passed on the fish. There were also raw vegetables, salami, cheese, rye bread, and a glass of tomato juice. At this time we were also given dessert. We ate everything except the fish, including the dessert.

After dinner the flight attendants came by with a large floral china teapot. It looked so out of place. It wasn't the normal stainless steel ones you see at home. Everyone was served a cup of coffee from the pretty teapot.

While waiting for my coffee I happened to glance around at the other passengers seated around us. Everyone still had their untouched desserts sitting on their trays. I sheepishly elbowed Jeff and pointed to everyone's desserts. We were so famished it didn't even cross our minds to wait for coffee to be served. I wanted to crawl under my seat. We must have looked like animals the way we inhaled our food. Jeff, being a guy, got over it pretty quickly and happily drank his coffee.

The flight to southern Russia was scheduled to be a two hour flight. It would be our final destination. We were in the air for about two hours when we started our descent.

We had heard several announcements over the loud speaker, all in Russian. They sounded normal enough, probably just arrival information I thought to myself.

Thankfully the landing was uneventful. There was no snow on the ground, but it was raining and dark outside. As we disembarked the plane I could see what looked to be a small airport. It wasn't lit up well, not the way most airports are. The buildings were different too. They were Quonset huts. There were no other airplanes around. It appeared to be a desolate airstrip. Only a few small lights lit up the building next to the tarmac.

As we headed down the passenger staircase, Nadia caught up with me. She immediately started apologizing. "Oh Michelle, I am so, so, soddy." She said this in her thick accent, with her adorable broken English.

I assumed she was apologizing for the scary take-off. She knew how I felt about flying. "Don't worry about it." I said, and asked her why she was apologizing.

"We are not where we are supposed to be." She said.

I started to panic. Asking her, "What? Why not? Where are we?" My mind was racing trying to figure out where in the world we were, and why she was so sorry.

During the flight we hadn't had any indication that we were landing somewhere else. What amazed me about the passengers was there was absolutely no indication of any kind of problem. No one was moaning about delays. There was no grumbling about landing in the middle of nowhere late at night. The people of this country took it in stride.

Nadia explained to me that there was too much fog to land at our destination, so we had to divert. "Where are we?" I asked her. She said we were about a three hour drive north of where we should be.

As I looked around and noticed how small the landing strip was, I was surprised we were able to land at all. I also wondered what we had been doing in the air for all that time. I was under the impression the whole flight shouldn't have taken more than two hours. Who knows, for all I knew we could have been over the Bermuda Triangle!

We felt helpless. It was scary to not have any idea where in a country you were. I don't know how people who choose not to use an adoption agency do this. At least we had a liaison with us for help.

Nadia went on to explain; because it was late there were no more flights for the evening. "I will call our driver and he will come get us." she said. "But it's the middle of the night, and it's a three hour drive in the rain." I exclaimed. I didn't want him to come all that way just for us. "Couldn't we just wait until morning for another flight?" I asked.

By this time Jeff had caught up to us and was up to speed on the situation. He also didn't want our driver, whom we had never met, to come all that way in the middle of the night just for us.

Nadia said it was no problem and he wouldn't mind at all. In fact, he was already on his way. *Wouldn't mind?* This was so foreign to us. Who in their right mind "wouldn't mind" leaving their cozy home to drive in the middle of fog and rain for three hours each way to pick up two strangers?

We would learn, throughout our journey, whether you are adopting in the United States or abroad, nothing ever goes as planned. The best thing you can do is not pour energy into trying to make things go perfect. The sooner you accept this fact the better off you will be.

We followed Nadia across the tarmac to an outdoor shelter to retrieve our luggage. Once we located all of our bags she led us through a tiny door into the Quonset hut. We were immediately greeted by two large Russian guards wearing fur hats and holding big guns. *Fantastic, I haven't had a panic attack for at least ten minutes!* Thankfully, they just wanted to see our passports before they let us in.

Once we were inside it was difficult to see. The large room was dimly lit with only a few household lamps. Nothing like an airport, but it did have a unique and inviting feel to it. There were a few benches for seating. The three of us made our way over and settled on one of the benches in a dark corner of the structure. I could hear the rain bouncing off of the tin roof. In some areas it was coming through the ceiling creating small puddles on the floor.

I noticed other passengers gathered in small groups, chatting quietly in various areas of the structure trying to keep warm. In one corner I noticed a group of Russian men passing around a flask. I imagine it had Vodka in it. I'm pretty sure it was the drink of choice here. It seemed most men drank it freely. I could tell, because I smelled it on the breath of several people in the shuttles and on the airplane. Even though many drank we never noticed anyone acting intoxicated or behaving badly. It seemed to be a way of life here. Come to think of it, I wondered if the pilot had been drinking. I didn't even want to go there. We were on solid ground now and I was grateful.

While Nadia and I got to know each other, Jeff found his own bench. It wasn't long before he was asleep. *How does he do that?!*

While she and I talked I realized how cold I was. There was no heat in the building. I tried my best to deal with it, but eventually I was miserable. It didn't seem to bother anyone else. I remembered the heat packets I had packed. I excused myself to rummage through my suitcase to find some. When I did I offered some to Nadia. She politely declined. She was used to the cold and didn't seem to mind it. Once I stuffed the small packets in my boots and gloves it didn't take long for my toes and fingers to become toasty warm.

As she and I talked, I took in all of the sights, sounds, and smells of the adventure we were on. I was surprised to see stray dogs and cats running around inside. At one point a cat came up to me and started rubbing up against my legs. Nadia ignored it. I figured she must not like cats. I leaned down to pet it. It seemed friendly enough. Nadia spoke up, "Please do not touch. Cats are veddy dangerous." I stopped out of respect for her, but in my mind wondered how they could be dangerous. They seemed so sweet. I read later that most stray cats in area we were in have rabies. Rabies was out of control in that region...*nice kitty!*

Jeff was over on his bench snoring away. I was sure everyone in the building could hear him. Nadia asked if I was hungry. I told her I was. She led me over to a deli counter which was lit by a single household lamp. There were a few tables set up where some of the stranded passengers were sitting. They were talking and sipping on hot drinks. As we approached the counter I could barely make out the contents. But, I could see the raw fish with the heads still attached. I politely declined the invitation to eat since it seemed that was all there was. "Are you sure?" asked Nadia. "Yeah, I'm sure. Thank you anyway." I said.

We walked back over to our bench. Jeff woke up long enough to ask where the bathrooms were. Nadia and I went back to talking.

Jeff came out of the restrooms motioning for me to come over to him. He told me all about the bathrooms, because he's a guy, and guys seem to love bathroom talk. In the men's room, instead of a toilet, was a hole in the ground. Next to the hole was a broom. It was there in case you missed the hole. I guessed we wouldn't be needing all of those travel size toilet seat protectors I brought with us.

It was about 1:30 in the morning when our driver, Dmitry, arrived to pick us up. He seemed to be in his early forties. He had a kind smile and spoke no English. He took my luggage and led us out to his car. Nadia got in the front seat with Dmitry. Jeff and I squeezed into the back. One of our suitcases had to be placed between Jeff and me in the back seat. I figured it might work as a makeshift airbag in the event of a collision.

The roads were wet and the fog was getting thick. These conditions didn't seem to faze our driver. He was driving pretty fast. It was probably because we were on an open highway with nothing around. I tried to get a look at his speedometer but it was in Kilometers and I didn't know how to convert that into miles per hour. Jeff looked at me and said, "Just go to sleep." I decided it would be best if I did. Naturally, Jeff started to doze off first.

While listening to the hum of the engine and the quiet chatter of Dmitry and Nadia speaking Russian, I finally drifted off to sleep.

It was still dark, and must have been the middle of the night, when we were awakened by the sounds of the engine slowing down. It was still quite foggy. We were in a desolate area. There was nothing around us as far as we could see. Dmitry pulled the car off of the road and onto a gravel driveway in front of a small structure. It had no markings. It appeared to be a house.

It was definitely *not* a hotel.

He shut off the engine and got out. Nadia stayed in her seat staring straight ahead, saying nothing. Panic surged through me. *Why would we be stopping here?* As Dmitry entered the building Jeff shot me a look that told me he was thinking the same thing. Before we left to come to this country we had been warned of kidnappings of Americans. Especially Americans who were adopting. The assumption was that if you are American and are adopting, then you must have money. This assumption could not be further from the truth.

As the minutes passed, the more nervous we became. We didn't bother to ask Nadia what was going on, we still didn't know her well enough to completely trust her. Several minutes later, Dmitry emerged from the building carrying a paper bag.

As he got into the car, he leaned over the back seat to hand us the bag. It was warm. Inside was a loaf of hot freshly baked bread and some raw almonds. He thought we might be hungry so he stopped to get us something to eat. I started crying for about the tenth time so far on this trip. We were humbled by their kindness and generosity. I also felt horrible for thinking the worst about them.

Fourteen

Ministry of Education

Through the darkness a town began to emerge. It would be our final destination. It was almost 4 a.m. when we arrived in the southern region of Russia near the border of Chechnya. At the time we had no idea of our proximity to this area.

Dmitry pulled off of the highway heading into town. He stopped the car in the loading area of the hotel where we would be staying. Nadia stepped out with us. She would be staying there too. We said our goodbyes to Dmitry and thanked him for driving all that way in the middle of the night. Nadia let us know we would see him again in the morning. I wanted to say, *you mean in a couple of hours!* Dmitry smiled warmly and drove away.

It was a nice hotel located in the center of the city square. The floors and walls of the lobby were decorated in marble. The subway and train stations in Moscow are famous for their use of it. Their stations are some of the most beautiful in the world.

The heat in the lobby felt pleasant. From what I could tell the heater in the car didn't seem to be working. I had trouble keeping warm during the last part of our journey. The packets in my boots were no longer giving off heat.

We were completely exhausted as we made our way down the hallway to our room. Nadia informed us of our meeting at the Ministry of Education at 9:00 a.m. She then asked what time we wanted our wake-up call. We told her 7:00, which would give us at least an hour to get ready. "Why you need call so early?" She asked. We explained that we wanted to shower. She abruptly replied, "I wake you up at 8:00. You no need shower. Americans take too many showers! I give wake-up call at 8:00." And just like that, she was gone, and the door to our room shut.

I was startled by her brazenness, but knew she meant no insult. Her abrupt statement regarding the wake-up call was clearly a cultural difference and not to be taken personally, which we didn't. Jeff and I already had a back-up plan in place. We would use our travel alarm clock. We would get about three hours of sleep.

Our room was clean and nicely decorated. It had twin beds and a television set. I noticed I was shivering again. The room was cold. I looked for a thermostat but there wasn't one, just some warm pipes running up the wall to the room above. Probably hot water pipes. I remembered reading in one of my books about this. In Moscow, the government controls the heat in the buildings, shutting it off during the appropriate seasons. I wondered if the same were true in the southern region. I never did find a thermostat.

There was a bathroom with a shower and a toilet. Thank you God! No hole in the ground here. I was thankful to have our own facilities. In Europe it is not uncommon to have community baths in hotels.

Located near the beds there was a small desk with a telephone on it. Oh, how I wanted to use that phone! I wanted to call my friends back home and tell them about our adventures in getting here. I also wanted to call my son whom I had never been that far away from. I already missed him. Using the phone was out of the question. Just one call would have costed us a small fortune. Our cell phones were not capable of being used in another country. We brought them anyway, an odd sense of security I guess.

We considered renting an international cell phone in case of an emergency. But after thinking more on it decided that there was no one we could call anyway. Calling 911 was an American calling feature. Besides, even if we could call someone for an emergency, we couldn't speak the language and we had no idea where we were. We would have to depend solely on God and the people He put in place to help us.

We were so exhausted we didn't have the energy to shower before going to bed. Sounds gross I know, but that's how tired we were! We set our alarm to wake us in a few hours.

The room was still dark when we were awakened to the sound of a loud telephone ringing. I jumped out of the bed and over to the desk to answer it, wondering who could be calling in the middle of the night. The female voice on the other end said something in Russian and hung up. I looked over at the clock. It read 8:00 a.m. "Oh no! We over slept!" I exclaimed, as I tried to figure out how that happened.

After a record setting morning of getting ready and only a few hours of sleep, we were ready to go when Nadia knocked our door. As I opened it, I was immediately struck by how fresh and beautiful she looked. She was on the same all-night journey we were and yet she looked amazing. I, on the other hand was haggard and my eyes were still bloodshot. I'm sure I looked as bad as I felt. We exchanged greetings as the three of us headed downstairs.

In the lobby we were introduced to a young well-dressed, woman in high-heeled shoes. Her name was Marina. She would be one of our interpreters during our time there. It was humbling to have this great group of people to help us. I was starting to realize the enormity of this endeavor. It made me think of just how many things were put into motion in so many people's lives on two continents, by a decision we made almost two years ago.

Dmitry was waiting in the car outside of the hotel. We wished he could speak English. We would have liked the chance to speak freely with him without the use of an interpreter all the time. I greeted him using my best Russian greeting as we piled into the car.

The drive through town reminded me of the older historical areas of our Eastern United States. Brick and plaster buildings, surrounded by wrought iron fences, lined the streets. I was secretly hoping we might stop to get a bite to eat since we hadn't had breakfast. It didn't happen and we didn't ask. We were obviously on a tight schedule. We were driven directly to the Ministry of Education office.

As soon as the car stopped Nadia and our interpreter took off walking fast, using that walk-run pace that Olga had used in the airport in Moscow. We were walking so fast we were practically running. I didn't think we were late, but kept up the best I could. Note to self, *take up jogging when we get home!*

I was nervous when we walked into the building. It was our first official meeting regarding the adoption held in their country. This meeting pertained to Anya. We would have other meetings in another area of the country for Svetlana. The girls were in two different orphanages. Svetlana's was several hours away.

I hoped I did not look as bad as I felt. We had been traveling for the last 48 hours, had little sleep, not much food, and were still on California time, which was currently the middle of the night.

We entered the office and were directed to sit down at a table where two women sat. One was an official who would decide if we could be considered adoptive parents, the other a nurse. We never did find out their names. If we did, we couldn't remember. Nadia sat on one side of us and our interpreter on the other. I was glad to have them both there. They were confident in their jobs and seemed to enjoy what they did.

As the meeting began I was so nervous I was sure everyone in the room could hear my heart beating. I was actually a little frightened at how hard my heart was beating, and for a moment wondered if anything was wrong with me. It certainly didn't feel normal.

Here we were in a foreign country in a government office, trying to convince them to allow us to bring two of their small citizens back to the United States to live with us forever. Who were we, that they would allow us such an honor?

We were asked a lot of questions about why we wanted to adopt. The meeting proceeded in the Russian language while our interpreter translated. While answering her questions I couldn't help but wonder if we were giving the right answers. What if something we said made them decide we weren't the right parents for these little ones?

During the interview I was able to recall something helpful for this meeting that will show you what a geek I am. It was something I learned from Star Trek. The episode involved an alien who could only communicate telepathically. The alien had an interpreter with him at all times to help him communicate with the lesser advanced species, known as humans. The humans made the mistake of directing their attention to the interpreter when speaking, instead of looking at the alien who was trying to communicate with them. It made the alien angry and he was greatly offended. Remembering this, I made sure to keep direct eye contact with whoever wanted information from us and not the interpreter. Being a huge fan of the show I was glad I was able to apply something I had learned to a real life situation. I'm not sure if it worked, but they seemed to appreciate it.

Next, it was the nurses turn to speak. As she read the report, we were able to hide our shock at the long list of health issues the child had, brain damage being one of them. Before we left on our trip, we were given a heads-up on the medical reports regarding children in orphanages. In Russia it was illegal for a foreigner to adopt a healthy child. Health reports were often exaggerated to help get the children out of the country more easily. The sicker they were, the more willing the Russian government would be to approve their adoption and let others take care of them. This relieved their country of the burden of cost and care for these children.

We were then given a turn to ask questions to both the nurse and the official. When there were no more questions we were handed documents to sign, requesting adoption in their country. There was only one problem…everything was written in Russian. Our interpreter paraphrased the wording for us, but how could we be sure that what she was telling us was true? For all we knew we could be signing our lives away.

It ended up coming down to one thing…faith. Faith in God, faith in our agency, and faith in the people who were hired to help us. We signed the papers and our meeting was over. We picked up our coats from the coatroom and sprinted back to the car where Dmitry was waiting. A new energy surged through us. Our next stop…to finally meet one of our possible future daughters!

Fifteen

Our First Meeting

We would just be visiting Anya that day, and Svetlana the next. It was a short drive across town to the first orphanage. Dmitry stopped the car in the parking lot of an old two-story brick building. It looked like it could be a school, or possibly an industrial building of some sort. We followed our coordinator and interpreter up the outside stairs of the building to an entrance where there was a metal door. Nadia pushed the buzzer to alert the staff that we had arrived.

Once inside, we made our way up a narrow set of stairs and down a series of long hallways. The building was old but clean. The smell of something cooking was overwhelming and attacked our senses. Whatever they were preparing didn't smell familiar or appetizing. I had been told by others who had adopted from this country that it was usually cabbage in some sort of broth. Caregivers serve it to the children because it is healthy and inexpensive.

As we continued to follow the woman who let us into the building,

Nadia and Marina picked up their usual quick pace. We passed by many rooms with closed doors. The only sounds we heard were the click-clack of our entourage's high heeled shoes on the linoleum floor. I thought it was odd that we neither heard, nor saw, any children. Especially since the building was so big. I just assumed we would have seen hundreds of children, or at least heard them.

We arrived at one of the closed doors and walked in. It was a playroom but there were no children inside. We were told by the woman to wait there. She walked out and closed the door behind her. I was shaking, this time it wasn't because I was cold. Jeff and I were super excited and nervous.

The waiting seemed almost unbearable. Then…the door finally opened. In walked a woman holding a baby in her arms. I immediately recognized Anya from her picture. Her big eyes and blond hair in the form of peach fuzz were unmistakable. Jeff and I were in awe as she entered the room.

As the woman who was carrying Anya walked towards me I opened my arms to her. Anya came to me unhindered and seemingly unafraid.

I held her as though it had always been that way. I knew in my heart that she was ours. I breathed in her smells and felt the softness of her skin against my cheek. It was almost like a dream. She didn't cry, but was extremely reserved, and cautious. She was rigid in my arms. Any sudden movement by anyone in the room caused her to jump. I had to remind myself, even though we felt as though we knew her, she had no idea who we were. To her, we were complete strangers.

I looked over at Jeff. He was smiling so big his eyes were practically popping out. He was just so incredibly happy! Anya kept looking over my shoulder with intense curiosity at him. Since men were generally not allowed in the orphanage, it was likely Jeff was the first man she had ever seen.

I held her for a while, but knew I needed to let him have a turn. I couldn't stand the thought of letting her go, even if it was for just a few minutes. She never made a sound as I gently handed her over to him. She stared at him as he held her. He held a toy out for her to take. She cautiously accepted it. After a few minutes her eyes moved around the room taking everything else in. We took as many pictures and videos of her as we could. We never wanted to forget that moment.

We tried hard at getting her to smile, but it was to no avail. There was a certain seriousness to her. We sat down on the floor so we could interact with her more freely. When I sat her down on the linoleum she became stiff, and almost fell over backwards. I caught her preventing her from getting hurt. We tried getting her to sit several more times. Worried she might get hurt, I placed her back in my lap. We were concerned that she could not sit up on her own, but knew that if there was something wrong with her we still wanted her to be ours, and would do whatever it took to get through it.

I looked her over making sure she was alright. Thankfully, she seemed somewhat healthy. There were no visible signs of abuse. We tried again to get her to interact with us. Still, her face was serious. She never made a sound.

I decided to try something a little more daring. I stood up and held her tightly under her arms. I lightly tossed her upward, like parents often do when they want to excite their children. Suddenly…she erupted in the heartiest laugh I had ever heard out of a baby! I kept it up. Going a little higher each time. Her laughter got louder and louder...pure joy! Not surprisingly, this child, not too many years later, would become my fearless daredevil, never getting enough of the big rollercoasters at any amusement park.

All too quickly, our visit was over. We wanted to stay longer but were told the children were kept on a strict schedule for naps and feeding times. It was time for her to nap. Our coordinator reassured us that we might be able to come back later in the day. We didn't want to leave but knew we had to comply with their wishes. As we said our goodbyes, Anya watched us intently over the shoulder of the orphanage director as she was carried away. The door closed behind them.

I was having a tough time with the fact that we had traveled for two days only to let her go after such a short visit. I had to remind myself, we were there just to get to know her. She really wasn't ours yet.

Our group headed back to the hotel around lunch time. Nadia and Marina had work to do so Jeff and I would be on our own for the rest of the afternoon. They gave us walking directions to the two restaurants in town that were close by. One had a menu written in English and served more home type cooking. The other was a cute little Italian place.

We decided on the restaurant geared more towards home cooking. I was craving a good salad. Since we had arrived, we had really only been eating beef jerky and the granola bars we brought with us. They were a gift from a friend back home who thought they would come in handy. They turned out to be a lifesaver on more than one occasion during our trip.

We made our way to the restaurant. The menu listed only one salad, a chicken Caesar. In the translation of the salad it was referred to as "lettuce with chicken chest." I never thought of chicken breast that way, kind of loses its appeal when you hear it described like that. I quickly lost my craving for the salad and chose cauliflower cooked in broth instead. It was the only other food I recognized. It tasted unusual but was satisfying.

Jeff and I spent the rest of the day touring the town square. We weren't sure of the importance of the historical monuments we saw because we weren't able to translate their descriptions.

A few blocks away we discovered the most beautiful church I had ever been in. As we walked inside the Russian Orthodox Church I made sure to cover my head with a scarf, as was the custom. There were floor to ceiling icons on the walls framed in what appeared to be pure gold. The walls were painted shades of turquoise and blues. There was a huge gold chandelier lined in candles which hung from the high domed ceiling. Sunlight from the outside filtered down through the windows of the dome onto a group of women singing "Ave Maria," a cappella style. They sounded like angels. It was in this sacred place where Jeff and I took a moment to praise and thank God for taking us on this incredible journey.

Sixteen

You Must Hide Evidence

It was still dark when I got out of bed the next morning. It was my 39th birthday. The trash truck behind the hotel had awakened us at 4:00 a.m. with its loud crashing and banging as the barrels were picked up and their contents dumped into the large empty metal containment portion of the truck. It sounded as though hundreds of empty glass bottles were being dropped into its bin. It was followed by a loud boom. The sound was excruciatingly loud, especially at that hour. The past two mornings the noise from this ritual shocked us into full consciousness. Once this happened there was little hope of trying to get back to sleep. I got out of bed.

As I turned on the faucet I wondered if there would be hot water. In this hotel there was about a fifty percent chance of getting hot water. I let the faucet run for a bit. Lukewarm was as hot as it was getting that day. It would have to be a fast shower.

By the time I was finished, Jeff was out of bed. We were dealing with an eleven-hour time change from what we were used to. In Russia it was early in the morning, and at home it was late afternoon. As far as our bodies were concerned it was almost dinner time.

I dressed quickly in an attempt to get warm. Jeff got into the shower and didn't give a second thought to the coolness of the water that was hitting him. That was, until it ran out. I heard him let out a scream. It was the last time for the duration of our stay that we would have hot water. I guessed we had gone over our allotment. If there was one.

It didn't seem to bother him much. I wish I was a little more care-free in life like he is. That's what I love about him. Most of the time he is a happy guy. I, on the other hand am the worrier. I am usually worried about something, everything, or nothing. Lately, as I grow in my walk with the Lord, I've been getting better about it. I am thankful He is patient with me.

Jeff was out of the shower and in the other room getting ready. The heat from my hair dryer felt good and was warming me up. While I was drying my hair, I thought about the day ahead. We were going to meet Svetlana! What an amazing birthday present.

I was completely lost in my thoughts when I heard a loud boom in front of me. I let out a scream. The room went dark. The noise was followed by a small flame which shot out of the electrical outlet where my blow dryer was plugged in. I stood there in disbelief, trying to process what had happened.

Jeff came running in. He examined the soot covered outlet. I started to panic. I really wasn't sure what went wrong, but knew it had something to do with my hair dryer. Being the worrier that I am, a hundred possibilities of what could possibly happen to me for destroying the electrical system in a hotel in a foreign country, shot through my mind. *What if the entire hotel was without power? How much damage did I cause? What if the hotel owners make us pay thousands of dollars to fix the damage?*

I sent Jeff down the hall to get Nadia. I told him to tell her exactly what had happened and to find out what we should do. A moment after he was gone, I thought, in my experience, whenever I ask Jeff to tell someone anything he tends to leave out all of the crucial details. In general men don't feel the need to disclose details like women do. With that in mind, I ran down the hall to tell her myself.

As I approached, I could hear him talking to Nadia at the doorway of her room, and as I suspected, he had simply told her we had no power. He did not disclose why. I stepped in and explained to her that my hairdryer had caused a power outage and it had scorched the wall where it was plugged in. Nadia looked me in the eyes, and replied very seriously in her Russian accent, "This is vedy bad." "You must hide evidence." *What?! Did I hear her right?!* What happened to the words "Don't worry, it will be ok." *Anything!* Except the words "hide evidence," and "vedy bad". All I kept thinking was, *what will they do to me if they find the evidence? And, who are we hiding it from?!*

Nadia called downstairs to the front desk to have an electrician come up to work on the problem. I wish I understood more of their language so I could have known what she told them. I was glad we were scheduled to be gone all day. I would not have to be interrogated by the hotel staff. Before we left the states I made sure to purchase a European adapter for appliances. I was using it at the time of the incident, so I have no idea what went wrong. We quickly got ready and left the room.

As the three of us exited the hotel, the cold air of that December day hit me. I shivered uncontrollably. For a moment I couldn't tell if it was because of the cold, my fear of what had just happened, or the excitement of the day ahead. It was probably all of those things.

Dmitry was waiting for us in the car out front. He got out and helped us with our things. I quietly and discreetly hid my hair dryer and the burned up adapter in the trunk of the car. I didn't want any "evidence" left in our room.

I greeted Dmitry by saying good morning in my best Russian, while making sure to pronounce the accent just right. He smiled warmly. "Dobroe utro" he replied. Which means, good morning. Once settled in the car, my fears melted away and were replaced with the excitement of day. We couldn't wait to meet Svetlana!

Seventeen

Meeting Svetlana

The morning was gray and overcast. We drove the narrow streets through the city towards the edge of town. The roads were lined with trees barren of their leaves, a reminder of winter.

At the edge of town was a small forest. The trees appeared to be Aspens. The sun was starting to come out. It was shooting gold beams of light down through the haze in between the trees. The beauty of this forest fascinated me. Winter hadn't completely taken over this land. We made our way out of the forest and onto the main highway. The countryside was a vast open expanse covered with rolling green hills. A small spattering of cows garnished the landscape. Our journey took us along the Caucasus Mountain range.

The busy two-lane highway seemed to be a main thoroughfare through the country. Once on the highway Dmitry picked up speed. He sped up the car as though we were once again late for something. He passed each slow moving vehicle as though he was a racecar driver on the Indy 500. I should have known he liked to drive fast, he was wearing an automotive racing jacket. With each car he passed he gave a look of satisfaction. It was as though he had just completed another lap on a high-speed track. I sat back and tried to relax.

The music playing on the car's CD player seemed to be calming me down. Dmitri always played music in the car. This particular score he had played before and I really liked it. It was powerful. Part of it was in a foreign language and part of it was in English. It might have been pop-opera. Whatever it was, it was absolutely beautiful. It was the perfect musical score for our journey which seemed to be more like a Hollywood movie. I wondered if he played this CD for all the Americans he drove for. I found out later, the name of the song was "Humilitas" by Lesiëm. The whole album was amazing.

The green hills eventually gave way to a flat, desert-like barren landscape. Every once in a while we would drive by a makeshift stand with a vendor selling items on the side of the road. As we flew by these stands, I tried to see what someone would be selling out there in the middle of nowhere. I was finally able to get a glimpse of one only to realize that they were dead animal carcasses hanging from poles. The only recognizable ones were the dead chickens. It was so cold outside that there was no need for refrigeration. Once again, I realized how lucky we were back home to have grocery stores with an abundance of beautifully packaged meat at our fingertips.

A couple of hours into the drive, Dmitry pulled the car off to the side of the road to one of these vendors. There was a man selling furs. He had them on display like clothes on a clothesline, using tree branches for posts. It was an odd site because there was nothing else around for miles. We learned the fur skins were used on the seats of cars to keep people warm while driving. During our stay we had noticed in all of the cars we had been in no one ever used their heater. At times it was like sitting in a refrigerator. We never said anything so as to not appear rude, but it was cold! My only guess was that it was too much work to remove heavy coats every time you got in and out of the car.

It felt good to get out and stretch our legs. The women chatted with the man selling the furs while the guys took a pit stop near some bushes.

When Dmitry came back he negotiated with the man for one of the furs. After some haggling he purchased one. He started to place it on the driver's seat of his car. Nadia started bickering with him. The animal skin had a horrible smell to it. She didn't want it in the car. As far as I knew the two of them were just colleagues, but they acted like an old married couple.

In battles pertaining to comfort during transportation, the woman usually wins. This culture was no different. Dmitry complied and put the smelly fur in the trunk.

We had driven for hours when we finally arrived at a small town near the base of the mountains. We drove up a dirt road where there were some small homes. Across from the homes was an old building. We had arrived at what was referred to as the "baby house." Instead of large buildings, known as orphanages, this part of the region used small homes for the children to reside. We were ushered into the orphanage director's office. She kindly greeted us in Russian.

Once we were seated, the director opened a file on her desk. It contained the medical report of Svetlana, who we were hoping to adopt. Our interpreter read the report to us. The baby was tiny for her age. They believed her to have been born premature. It was reported, that she also, had some sort of "brain damage." She had been in the orphanage since she was released from the hospital, a few months after her birth, where she was being cared for due to her premature size.

The whole time the director was reading the medical report, I couldn't help but notice Jeff dancing around in his seat and unable to sit still. I tried to ignore him. I didn't want to draw attention to whatever was going on with him, but it was really annoying. Once the director finished reading the report, she handed it to us to look over and asked if we had any questions.

Jeff spoke first…"Can you tell me where the bathroom is?" is the first thing that came out of his mouth. *Wow.*

The director obliged. Someone showed him where he could go to relieve himself, which turned out to be an outhouse out in the yard.

Once Jeff was finished and came back into the office, it was time to meet Svetlana. A woman entered the room carrying a small baby wrapped in winter clothes and wearing a knitted hat. There was no doubt that this was the baby whose picture I had been carrying around since we had first heard of her.

Peeking out from the layers of wool clothing was a set of sad looking eyes. The woman who carried her into the office removed the baby's coat and hat. She then took her over to the director's desk and plopped the baby down on its surface. As we stared in awe at this precious sight, the director looked at us, while gesturing with her hands, from the baby to us, and said in her broken English, "You want??" Russians are so direct. "Yes, yes!" was our response. The director motioned to us that it was ok to pick her up. The baby was not happy and began to cry. Understandably so. It had to be scary for her. We were strangers.

Even though she was crying, she felt so perfect in my arms. She was so little. After a little while, I handed her to Jeff who took her into his arms. I could tell immediately he was in love with this kid. The smile on his face was huge. He rocked her, trying to console her while she cried. He talked to her and gave her a rattle to play with. She was terrified but eventually calmed down.

After about fifteen minutes we were told that it was her nap time and they had to take her away. I didn't want to leave. We had flown halfway around the world and just driven three hours across the country to see her, only to spend fifteen minutes with her. It all seemed so unfair. Yet, we understood that if we wanted to adopt this child, then we had to play by their rules. We thanked the director for her time, and then reluctantly headed back to the car where Dmitry was waiting.

Once again we flew down the main highway of the country, this time the opposite direction of the baby we had waited so long to meet. I couldn't stop thinking of her. I had only held for such a short time. I wanted to hold her and protect her for the rest of her life. I imagined what our lives would be like with her and couldn't wait for the day when we could bring both of the girls home with us. My heart already ached.

The car ride was long. This time Jeff sat in the front seat with Dmitry, while the women sat in the back seat. It would be a few hours before we were back at the hotel. Jeff and I were starving. The people we traveled with never stopped to eat. Probably because there were no places to eat. There were no fast food restaurants in this part of the country, only petrol stations. We hadn't eaten since the flight the day before.

Jeff took out the beef jerky and granola bars we had brought with us. He offered to share our snacks with our group. The women politely declined. Dmitry was happy to try some of the beef jerky. He liked it a lot. He and

Jeff shared the bag. Even through the language barrier they had found something in common. We made a mental note to bring some back with us on our second trip, just for Dmitry.

Dmitry dropped us off in front of our hotel. As I got out of the car he handed me the CD we were listening to, the one I really liked. Nadia told me he wanted me to have it for my birthday. I was deeply touched, especially since it seemed to be his favorite music.

Jeff and I went back to our room to wash up a bit. He was taking me to dinner for my birthday to the Italian restaurant in town.

The outlet in the bathroom of our room was no longer black with soot. It must have been changed out while we were gone. Nothing was ever said regarding what happened.

Just before we left, Nadia came by our room. She brought me a bouquet of tulips. It was very thoughtful. I thanked her for being so sweet. From the time we spent together, and this kind gesture, I could tell she was a good person. I looked forward to hanging out with her on our daily excursions. If only she lived in the United States, I could see us becoming friends.

The restaurant was within walking distance of our hotel. The menu was in Russian, but since Nadia knew we were planning to go, she had our interpreter write down the names of some of my favorite dishes on a piece of paper so I could hand it to the waiter.

We ended up ordering their house pizza. It arrived, thin crust style, almost like a cracker, no sauce, but a lot of cheese. It was topped with pomegranate seeds. Surprisingly, it tasted good.

As we walked back to our room after dinner, I was amazed that God had given me the greatest birthday ever!

Eighteen

Being Detained

The week was filled with official business, more visits to the orphanage, and some sight-seeing.

On our last visit to Anya's orphanage we were ushered to a different room to spend time with her. It was set up like the living room of a home. It was there where we finally saw some other children.

In the center of the room was a makeshift playpen made of plastic panels. It was just like the ones pet stores use for puppies. This one was filled with approximately ten crawling babies, all appearing to be about a year old.

An orphanage caregiver was sitting nearby at a computer desk with her back to them. The babies were piled one on top of each other, trying desperately to climb over the side of the pen. The weakest on the bottom, the strongest on top. All were crying or screaming, trying to get the caregiver's attention. She was ignoring their screams to be held. I knew she had to. There was only one of her and roughly ten of them. There was no way she could tend to emotional needs of all of them.

Looking in the pen, I couldn't tell them apart. They all appeared identical because of their shaved heads. And all of them were wearing mostly the same clothing. I asked Jeff to help me figure out which one was Anya. He walked over and easily pointed her out.

I lifted her up and out, feeling bad for not being able to hold all of them. The cries from the other babies grew louder as I carried her over to a rocking chair.

Anya was much more social with us on this visit. She was comfortable and playful in her surroundings. I guessed this was probably the room she spent most of her time.

We were pleased to see her walking with the aid of a walker. She happily entertained herself with various toys around the room. We surmised that her stiffness on the first day we met her was probably a defense mechanism. We had no more concerns over the supposed "brain damage" written on her medical report.

Our visit to the orphanage had come to an end. It would be the last time we would get to hold Anya until the judge allowed us to come back to Russia. The time period for our return was unknown. It was completely up to the judge and the powers that be. We would have to go back home and wait for approval to come back.

Russian law required two visits to their country in order to adopt their children. It was hard leaving the girls behind. Everything in our being told us they were already ours. I held Anya as long as I could. Nadia told us it was time to leave. I placed her down amongst her toys and reluctantly walked out the door. I prayed for God to keep her safe.

We woke up early for our flight headed to Moscow. The sun had not yet come up, but I could already tell it was freezing outside. We sat with Nadia in the warmth of the hotel lobby waiting for Dmitry to arrive. Jeff and I were tired and hungry. We already missed the girls. It didn't seem right not taking them home with us, but it was out of our hands.

In the lobby was a small café. I spotted some bread in the glass case at the counter. I pointed to one of the plain rolls. "Please." I said in Russian to the lady. She told me how much. I counted out the appropriate amount of Rubles, saying thank you as I handed them to her. My stomach was growling as I walked back to the bench to where Nadia was sitting. I took a bite, and almost gagged. Inside the roll was some sort of mystery meat. It had a horrible smell and taste to it.

I showed it to Nadia and asked her what was inside. She simply replied, "Don't eat any of the meat here." She didn't elaborate. I never did find out why or what it was. I was always a borderline vegetarian. This trip had pushed me closer to actually being one. I walked over to the trashcan and threw out the mystery roll, my stomach still growling.

Dmitry picked us up for the last time on this trip. The drive to the airport was not long, which was nice for a change. I asked Nadia if we should bring car seats for the girls when we come back to get them. She replied, "What is car seat?" She had no idea what one was. I took that as a "no" to our question. Besides, there were no seatbelts in the back seats of any of the cars. How would we have secured them?

We arrived at the airport just as the sun was starting to show its brilliance in the sky. From the outside, the building looked normal enough. It was like any other airport. Inside, was much different.

There were guards wearing dark green military outfits, they were wearing ushankas on their heads. Ushankas are the fur hats commonly seen on Russian people during the winter. The guards were heavily armed. Each holding a large automatic weapon in their hand, and a pistol on their waist belt. We were ushered into a line for passport control.

At this point in our travels we were exhausted and homesick. I wasn't thinking about things you do, and don't do, that go against someone's culture.

While standing in line to go through passport control, I noticed one of the armed guards was staring at me. It was making me nervous. I made the mistake of smiling at him. I didn't mean anything by it. It's just what I do when people are looking at me. However, in their culture, smiling has a completely different meaning than in America.

The guards immediately pointed to Jeff and me, directing us out of the line. Nadia walked over with us. She told us the guards wanted to see our passports.

They must have known we weren't from the area. My heart was pounding. I tried telling myself not to worry. After all, we had the appropriate documents to exit the country and get back home.

After the first guard examined our passports he showed them to another guard. We were then pulled aside. The two guards spoke to us sternly in Russian. We didn't have a clue what they were saying but we could tell they were questioning us.

I looked over to Nadia for some answers. She explained that we needed to show the guards our "travel vouchers." We had never heard of this type of document, but to appease the guards, we searched through our papers, thinking perhaps we had them and they were called something else. We couldn't find what they were referring to.

The guards were now demanding these vouchers. We frantically pulled out all of the papers we had, showing them to Nadia, who in turn handed them to the guards. None of documents we had were what they were looking for. They were losing patience with us.

The guards reprimanded us in Russian. They were very angry. We had no idea what they were saying. I was getting scared. I started pulling out our adoption papers, thinking maybe if they knew we were here on adoption business, they would let us go. Nadia quietly told us to put them away.

She then turned towards us…now *she* was asking us for our travel vouchers. *I thought she was on our side!* She should know all of the documents we were hand carrying. If we needed something more, she would have told us…*right?*

The guards were getting louder with us. Nadia seemed more and more frustrated. She started arguing with the guards. Oh how I wish I spoke fluent Russian! She asked us again, and again for these papers. *How many times did we need to tell these people?! We didn't have them!* After several more minutes of interrogation by all three of them, Nadia told us to wait there. She and the guards disappeared into a room taking our passports and visas with them.

To describe our feelings at that moment as being terrified would be an understatement. When it came to getting back home, I used to feel somewhat safe because I knew we had the appropriate paperwork. I even slept with my passport attached to my hidden money belt.

Now, with those papers no longer in our possession, Jeff and I were at the mercy of this government, and the two angry guards. *Was Nadia really on our side?* I had to wonder. She seemed as frustrated with us as the guards were.

Jeff and I stood there frozen in time. We didn't dare move from the very spot where they told us to wait for them. Every part of me was shaking in fear. Our constitutional rights didn't mean anything here. I started imagining the worst. I had watched too many television shows where innocent people had been locked up in other countries for things they were ignorant to.

I started to pray hard. I began to feel the presence of Jesus. I could almost visualize him in my mind, standing behind us. His hands on our shoulders, saying, *I am with you.* I was still scared, but took comfort in knowing Jesus was there too.

Nadia and the guards were still in the room. The door was shut so we couldn't see what was going on. For all we knew, they were going to arrest us.

While we were standing there, for what seemed like hours, I spotted Dmitry. He seemed to know people at this airport. It was that way through the whole trip. He always happened to run into someone he knew. I kept a close eye on him. He was the only familiar thing we knew, and we felt we could trust him. If something happened to us maybe he could help. I watched as he smiled and hugged people.

Eventually, Nadia and the guards emerged from the room. As they walked towards us their facial expressions revealed none of them were happy. I wondered what they would do to us.

Nadia spoke first. She informed us that we were never to come through there again without our travel vouchers. And, that the guards were letting us go. I thought to myself, *don't worry, we weren't coming back through this airport ever again.* We would figure out another way, by train perhaps.

The guards gave us more stern warnings. We kept our heads low and gave our most humble apologies. Even though we still didn't understand what we did or didn't do.

The next line was to check our baggage. The four of us, Dmitry included, were herded through a narrow doorway into a room about the size of my bathroom. There was a counter where two female officials stood. They didn't look happy either. They were the baggage controllers. There were about twenty other people in this room. The air was hot and stuffy. I thought I was going to faint. We still had on our heavy coats. It was too difficult to carry them, and our baggage, so we left them on.

I looked to my right and noticed an old antique scale. It was similar to one you would find at a carnival, like the ones they use to guess your weight. *Wow, that thing is old!* I thought to myself. As soon as the thought crossed my mind someone picked up my suitcase and set it on the old scale.

One of the women behind the counter spoke up gruffly in Russian. Nadia started arguing with her. *Here we go again.* This was the first time I had seen Nadia really mad. And then, out of nowhere, I heard Dmitry speak up. He started arguing with one of the baggage controllers. He was angry and got loud with her. This surprised both of us. We didn't think he had a mean bone in his body. He was normally quiet.

The arguing went on for a few minutes while Jeff and I stood there. Again, not having a clue as to what was going on. Nadia told me to give her my money, our bags were too heavy and they were charging us. I didn't argue. I just asked, "How much?" She gave me an amount in Rubles. I pulled out several bills trying to fish for more. She took it. She told me to put the rest away, as if to say, they aren't getting one cent more. I couldn't compute fast enough in my brain as to how much it was in American dollars, nor did I care. I would have given them everything just to get on that airplane.

All through baggage control, Nadia kept telling me over and over not to worry. She could see the fear on my face and knew I was terrified. The woman behind the counter accepted our money and it was done.

Nadia explained later that she and Dmitry were mad because the baggage controllers were clearly taking advantage of us. It made us feel good that they fought so hard for us, yet confused by her behavior during the incident with the guards. I guessed she needed to play along with them in order to get us out of there, which we were grateful for.

We were pushed by the throngs of people through to the next room. I sensed we were getting closer to freedom. It was so crowded that everyone was pressed up against each other. Americans are used to our personal space. These types of situations make us uneasy, but in most European countries their citizens are not bothered by issues of space. It is a way of life for them.

I spotted Dmitry near the door of the room. He appeared to be leaving. I asked Nadia where he was going. She told me he was not able to go any further with us. "But I didn't get to say goodbye, or even thank him for all he had done." I said, my voice crackling while fighting back the tears. I was still shaken from our encounter with the guards and the scary baggage ladies. Now, Dmitry was leaving us. We had formed a friendship with him and I didn't know if we would ever see him again. I asked Nadia to tell him goodbye for us and to thank him for everything. She said she would tell him when she talked to him. For me, it didn't seem enough to have to relay such a heartfelt message, but there was little choice so we pressed on.

The next room we were pushed into was a bit larger. It had big windows. We were able to see outside to the airfield. We were getting closer!

We were still pressed up against all of the other people like cattle waiting to go through the gate. There must have been fifty people in this room, but it was so quiet you could hear a pin drop.

Another cultural thing I noticed while on our journey…while waiting, people didn't make small talk with strangers. I had yet to hear anyone complaining about things such as long lines, stifling air, or standing for long periods of time. The people there were quiet and stone faced as they stared out the windows. Most were in dark clothing and almost all of them wore hats. A different way of life than we were accustomed to. It seemed very 1950's.

I was uncomfortable with how quiet it was. It was probably the reason I felt the need to open my big mouth and say something to Jeff. It wasn't anything more than small talk. I tried to speak quietly, but it was loud enough to make all fifty people in that room turn around and look at us as though we had two heads. I realized they were staring, because up until that point, they hadn't known we were foreigners. The locals weren't used to hearing anyone speak English. Foreigners were rare in that part of the country.

We had run into a similar situation earlier in the week at the internet café. Jeff and I were at a computer sending e-mails. We had asked the person who was monitoring the café to switch the keyboard symbols to English. Others heard us. Pretty soon, Jeff and I had about five young men, appearing to be in their early twenties, hovering over us, watching us type letters to home. They were absolutely fascinated by the fact that we were from America. They never spoke to us. They couldn't due to the language barrier. They just hung over us, watching intently.

The situation in the airport reminded me of an old commercial I used to see on television. The one where someone standing in a crowded busy room opens his mouth to speak. Everyone drops everything to look at him to hear what he has to say. I didn't say another word and hoped everyone there would forget I existed. I also didn't want to get into any more trouble than we had gotten into in the last couple of hours. I just wanted to go home!

We were finally ushered outside. The fresh cold air felt amazing. Even though this was the same type of older plane we flew on before, the one I thought I was going to die on, my perspective had changed. I could not wait to get on board. Better to take my chances in the air than to possibly get arrested for something I didn't understand I was doing wrong.

As we walked across the tarmac I picked up the pace a bit. I wanted on that plane more than anything. Nadia gently grabbed my arm and pulled me back. She told me that traditionally men board first. *You have got to be kidding me?!* I sent Jeff on ahead. He was clueless to all of this as he ascended the stairs to the aircraft, leaving me behind.

For the first time on our journey I was truly homesick. I was tired of not knowing what to do to please people. I was frustrated by not being able to understand anyone or communicate our needs without the use of an interpreter. I could not imagine how hard it must be for immigrants coming into our country. They must feel some of the same frustrations.

The women were finally allowed to board and the plane took off without incident. Once airborne, I breathed a huge sigh of relief. My perspective of that rickety old plane we flew on the first time had changed. This airplane, which in my mind, was once an old heaping mass of metal on which I was sure I would die, was now our glorious rocket to freedom!

Nineteen

Exhausted and Homesick

During the flight I spoke with Nadia about our return trip to Russia. I never wanted to have to deal with the guards at that airport again. I asked her about taking a train the next time from Moscow to southern Russia. She told me it would take days to go by train and it wasn't safe. Basically, the answer was no. It made me sick to my stomach to think we might possibly be detained again when we returned.

The rest of the flight to Moscow was a blur. Now that we weren't spending any more time with the girls, Jeff and I wanted nothing more than to get back home. Landing in Moscow made us happy to have made it so far, yet sad at the same time. We were getting further away from the girls.

Our driver picked the three of us up from the airport. It was much colder than where we just were a few hours ago. It was also gloomy. The streets were wet with the melting snow, which had now turned a charcoal color from being shoveled around.

We piled into the car. This time the mood was much different than it was the first time we arrived in this city. Jeff and I were emotionally and physically drained. The exhaustion I felt was like none I had ever felt in my life. Jeff felt it too. As the car bumped around the streets of the city, Jeff and I could hardly keep our eyes open. We tried hard to stay awake to be polite, but it was literally impossible, and we quickly succumbed to our fatigue.

We woke up when our driver arrived at Nadia's apartment to drop her off. We said our goodbye's, not knowing how long it would be before we would see her again.

At the hotel we thanked our driver for the ride, and then he too was gone. As we stood in the hotel lobby, a feeling of loneliness washed over us. It sounds strange to be lonely on the trip of a lifetime, but there it was. I longed for home. The language barrier had been exhausting, and being detained shook us up pretty bad. One thing I was not prepared for was the emotional roller coaster we rode on a daily basis.

There was only one departing flight a day from Moscow to New York. Our flight didn't leave until late the next day. It was booked that way in case there were any delays in getting back to Moscow.

The hotel looked normal enough. The lobby was modern and nicely decorated. The woman at the front desk was friendly and spoke some English, which was a relief. She checked us in, and then directed us to a security gate to get to our rooms. There was a very large unfriendly man in charge of the security gate. He let us through without any issues.

Once we got past the security guard, the décor had changed so much we thought we were in another building, only we weren't. The hotel was old and in need of repairs. There were several young women, and some men, hanging out in the hallway. Some of them had their arms wrapped around each other. Others were engaged in different types of flirtatious behavior. We made our way past the "ladies" in the hallway. They seemed oblivious to us.

We found our room and quickly locked the door behind us. Our room was decorated with 1950's style furniture, including twin beds. The air was stifling. It felt like someone had left the heater on high. We looked around for a thermostat but there wasn't one. Jeff tried to open a window, but it wouldn't open. Cigarette smoke poured in through the heating vents making our eyes burn. Out in the hallway we could still hear squeals and giggles from the people standing out there.

I was so tired I couldn't even stand up anymore. I was scared of being in this place and wished our flight was that same day so we just could go home. Being away for two weeks seemed like a month.

Jeff and I collapsed on the beds. We were too tired to undress. It was still daylight. We could hear the sounds of a jackhammer. It was incredibly loud and must have been close by, if not inside the hotel. It didn't seem to matter because we fell fast asleep.

The room was dark when I woke up. I was in a daze. It took me a moment to realize we were still in the hotel room in Moscow. As I lay there unsure of how long we had been asleep. Jeff also started to wake up. Things seemed to have quieted down in the hallway and I could no longer hear the sounds of the jackhammer. We were both starving. I honestly couldn't remember the last time we ate.

We got up and found our way to a tiny café in the hotel. There was only enough room for three tables. It was cozy and the lighting was dim. There were a few men sipping on hot drinks. We made our way to an open table.

We ordered soup from the menu. We ate but could barely keep our eyes open. We figured it was the middle of the night. Once we were finished eating, we made our way to our room and immediately fell back to sleep.

Sometime later, when we awoke for the second time, we were both disoriented, not quite sure of where we were or what time it was. Was it day or night? I looked at my watch and then outside. It was daylight, but hard to tell if it was early morning or early evening. It was overcast so I couldn't see the sun. As I adjusted to my surroundings, and kept looking at my watch to figure out if it was am or pm, I realized that it was the afternoon of the next day. We had slept for sixteen hours! Luckily, we had not missed our flight. We washed up, brushed our teeth, and left the hotel. I couldn't wait to get out of there!

We arrived at the airport in plenty of time for our evening flight, although, we no longer had an interpreter or coordinator to help us navigate the Moscow airport. There weren't any signs in English and we didn't know where to go.

We happened to notice a few other American couples who looked as lost as we were. We introduced ourselves. It turned out they were also adopting. We wandered around together, all of us confused as to where to go. Other Americans joined us, including the couple we met in line at passport control when we first arrived in the country. We naturally formed a circle in the middle of the bustling airport as we took turns sharing our travel adventures.

We shared stories of our travels and food experiences. All of us had lost weight. One couple had spent the week with a host family who weren't very nice to them. The husband literally starved all week because he couldn't stomach any of the food being served to him. We seemed to be the fortunate ones by having a restaurant nearby.

One couple had traveled near the area where we had been. They had seen trains left on the tracks that had been blown up by terrorists. We talked about the children we met and how hard it was to leave them behind. Those of us who had pictures shared them.

It was nice to be able to communicate freely in English. There really wasn't anyone to just chat with for the past week. Nadia said it was exhausting to try to speak English, and I felt the same about trying to speak Russian. It wasn't like Spanish where some of the words are recognizable. The Russian language made your jaw hurt because you were using muscles you didn't normally use. I did find it a beautiful language, and would have liked to have learned more, but it was difficult to learn quickly.

Our next two flights home were long and uneventful. It felt good to be back in the states. I felt safe once we were on American soil. Our total travel time to get home to San Diego was around twenty four hours. Jeff had to be at work within a couple of hours of us arriving. He couldn't use any more of his vacation days. He had to save them for our return trip to Russia.

Once Jeff left for work, I made a run to Walmart to pick up some things we needed for the house. As I entered the store, a large American flag hanging from the ceiling caught my eye. I had never noticed it before. I stood there staring at it, in awe of its symbolism. I began to cry. I was so thankful to God for everything He brought us through. But mostly, I was grateful to be able to live in this beautiful free country of ours.

Twenty

Waiting...

Christmas was different this year. It wasn't the same now that we knew what we were missing, which was two little ones. We didn't put a tree up that year. There wasn't a whole lot of time since we had just come home. January was a blur, as was most of February, with no word as to our return date.

Before we could return to Russia we had another mountain of documents to complete. Our fingerprint records and health exams still needed to be updated every three months. We were also required to meet with a psychologist. It was to make sure we were competent to raise a child. It's a good thing you don't need psychological clearance *while* you are raising a child! I don't know many parents who would pass.

Each time we completed a document it then had to be notarized and apostilled, making it recognized in a foreign country. By the time our adoption was completed, our notary fees alone were close to $3,000.

Life turned into a waiting game. The time to return to officially adopt the girls was unknown. It was in the hands of God and the Russian government.

During this time of waiting, friends dropped off donations for us to take back with us and deliver to the orphanage. The babies there were in desperate need of cloth diapers, rash cream, and medicines of different varieties. We filled two suitcases with donations from friends. February came and went…

It wasn't until March when we finally received a call from the agency with a return date. We would be heading back to Russia in April. Right around Easter! The government had approved our request to adopt the girls. Four months after we had met them, we would be allowed to go before the judge, who would then decide if they could officially be ours.

We felt in our hearts the girls were already ours. Waiting for someone else to decide their fate, and ours, was especially difficult. What if the judge said no? We put those feelings aside and put faith forward.

Our agency began travel arrangements. We would need an open airline ticket for our return home. In most adoption cases in Russia, the judge decides how long the prospective parents should stay in their country, in order to bond with the children before getting to take them home. It could be anywhere from ten days to three weeks. Our agency director informed us that if all went well, we would be bringing the girls home right around Easter.

During our last trip, while waiting to fly home to California, I remembered sitting in JFK Airport, thinking about my extended family. They were only an hour drive from where we were. I really wanted to visit them. We were on such a tight schedule at that time that it just wasn't possible. I come from a big Italian family. I had two grandmothers still alive, several cousins, aunts, and uncles, all in Pennsylvania. We are a close family.

I knew on this trip, on the return flight, we would once again have a layover in New York. With this in mind, while making plans for our second trip to Russia, we also made arrangements to extend our return layover and completely surprise my family with our new family members. This plan would help keep me even busier, making the time pass more quickly.

It was a Saturday…There were only eight days left until we were leaving to finalize the adoption. My son Sean and I were out running errands. We had some last minute things to get done since Jeff and I would not be home for a while.

While we were sitting at a red light my thoughts were on Sean and how much I would miss him while we were gone. I suddenly snapped to when the car behind me slammed into us. No one was hurt, but there was significant damage to my car. This was not what we needed right now. It would be one more thing we would have to deal with before we left.

Monday morning…before I even opened my eyes, I could feel the soreness in my throat and the stuffiness in my nose. *This can't be. I can't be sick now!* I had only one week left at my job before I was on leave, for at least six weeks. Being self-employed it was crucial for me to work as long as I could before we left.

I have often criticized people who go out in public when they are sick. I felt they should stay home, instead of exposing others to whatever ailments they have. Now here I was, doing the same thing. I showered and dressed, then took some daytime cold medicine in an attempt to mask my symptoms. I got in the car and headed for work.

Between my conscience, and the fact that I was feeling awful, I only made it halfway before I turned the car around and went back home. I cancelled my day and hoped my clients would understand.

Once I got home I wanted nothing more than to crawl into bed. But, something kept nagging at me to have my fingerprints scanned. It was something we had to do every three months. It was so authorities would have a current record of whether or not we had committed a crime. This was part of the adoption process. My fingerprint records were due to be updated before we left. I was going to have them done on Thursday, but something kept nagging at me to take care of it that day instead of waiting.

I got back in the car, still feeling awful. I drove downtown to the federal building to fill out the paperwork to have my prints updated.

Once I was in the building I got the typical run around, which is common in all government agencies. I was sent from floor to floor for the necessary papers. It seemed no one who worked there knew where I was supposed to go to fill out these papers. During the running around from floor to floor I was getting weaker and weaker. At one point I stopped to lean up against a wall. I felt myself getting lightheaded and felt as though I was going to faint. I guess I was sicker than I thought. I was able to find some water and took some deep breaths to regain my strength.

After searching the building, I finally found the office where I needed to fill out the documents, only to find out that I had to drive to another building to have the fingerprints actually scanned. I felt like a rat in a maze.

I managed to drive to the next place I needed to be. As I entered the building, I was shocked to see how many people were waiting. There was no way I would be able to wait around for what might be hours. My symptoms were getting worse and I could barely stand up. I just wanted to go home and go to bed, but something inside was urgently telling me there was no time and I needed to do it right then. I listened to that inner voice and took a number. I found a chair, and tried not to breathe on anyone. I felt bad for the people sitting next to me and prayed they would not get what I had. While waiting, I prayed continually for strength.

Three hours later, my number was called and I was able to complete the task. I drove home and went straight to bed, sleeping until the next day.

The next morning I woke up feeling a lot better. Until…I got a call from the agency saying that some of our documents were filled out incorrectly. The documents had to be re-done. I had a few hours on Thursday to take care of it, which was the day I was going to get my fingerprints scanned, until I had that nagging feeling to get them done on Tuesday. I was glad I listened to the voice inside of me. It took all of my free time on Thursday to have the papers re-done correctly.

That week was rough. I still wasn't feeling good. We were low on funds and we still had to deal with getting the car fixed. Not to mention, my fear of flying and being so far away from my son. Jeff and I argued a lot that week. We were exhausted and emotionally done. It was moments like those when seeds of doubt would work their way in to my mind. The fear I was feeling over all of the possible things that could go wrong was eating away at me.

Twenty-one

The Warning

The excitement over the news that we would be returning to Russia quickly turned to panic and despair.

We had received an e-mail from the American Embassy. It was a warning. The area near the Chechnya border, which is where we were going to be, was turning into a political hotspot. Embassy workers in the area were being pulled out. There were military clashes, kidnappings of aid workers, and foreigners. Muggings and violent crimes were on the rise. We were strongly advised to cancel our trip. The warning stated there would be no help or protection for us if something went wrong.

This was one of the areas I had seen on the news almost two years ago. I remembered thinking to myself back then; the odds of us going to a terrorist region were slim. Those odds were smaller than I thought.

My heart sank. *How could this be happening?!* I immediately thought of Svetlana and Anya. *What if they were in danger? We couldn't just leave them there!*

In our hearts they were already our daughters. We needed to bring them home. But, how could we purposefully fly into an area where there was a civil war going on? Would the government even allow us to? The panic and tears came like a river.

I called Jeff at work to give him the grim news. He couldn't say much. He was too stunned to say anything, and he was in front of customers. He told me to pray, it was out of our hands. We would talk later when he got home.

I hung up and prayed hard. I asked God what to do. I begged Him for answers. He seemed silent. I relayed our latest update to some close friends asking them to pray for direction.

I spent most of the day pacing and praying until Jeff finally came home from work. We sat down to discuss the situation. We didn't know what to do. At this point, we couldn't imagine our lives without the girls. I also had my son, Sean, to think about. If something happened to us, how would it affect him?

That evening we talked it over with Sean. We explained the dangers involved, making him aware of the risk. As a family we also discussed what kind of future the girls would have if they stayed in Russia. It would have been bleak, especially in a war zone. They might never get adopted by another family. We couldn't even bring ourselves to entertain the thought of them going to another family. Even though the adoption wasn't final, we had already bonded with them. As far as we were concerned, they were our kids. We loved them.

After discussing the different possibilities of the situation, it was decided by the three of us. We would continue to move forward to bring the girls home.

We chose not to tell the rest of our families, and most of our friends, about the warning. It would not only upset them, but they might try to talk us out of it. A scripture came to mind, *"Fear of man will prove to be a snare, but whoever trusts in the Lord is kept safe."* Proverbs 29:25 (NIV)

Over the next couple of days there were signs, literally everywhere, that seemed to confirm our decision. One of many was while I was driving to work was a billboard that read, "The anecdote to fear is action."

Another one was about three days before the e-mail from the Embassy. It was an e-mail from my dear friend, Linda. She sent me a story on trusting God. So much was going at the time that I had forgotten all about it.

Linda and I were getting together the morning after we received the Embassy e-mail. I knew her well enough to know she wouldn't judge us for our decision to go to back to Russia at such a dangerous time so I shared the e-mail warning with her.

She asked me if I remembered the e-mail she sent me about faith and the rope. The story talked about trusting God no matter what the circumstances are. Even if the "rope" we have is attached to our waist and is keeping us from falling. If God tells you to cut the rope, then you do it. Linda looked at me with tears in her eyes and said, "Cut the rope!" Then she said, "Go get those babies!" It was clear to us what we should do. Having the support of our close friends meant a lot to us and helped us get through the tough times.

The story she sent me is titled "The Rope Story of the Mountain Climber" I have searched the internet dozens of times, and written e-mails, trying to find the author. It always comes up "Anonymous." Unfortunately, I legally could not include the story in this book without permission. I feel strongly that the story is meant for many people to hear, and I highly recommend doing a search on the internet to read it for yourself. You can

Google it with the words "The Rope Story tells of a mountain climber…" Dozens of websites should come up that have used this story of faith on their pages.

Now that the decision was made to go through with our plans to bring Anya and Svetlana home, our house was abuzz with activity making final preparations for our new family members.

Our agency was able to give us a bit of a timeline for our trip but we would still need an open ticket to fly home. If the judge allowed us to come home right after our court date in Russia, then it would put us back in New York the day before Easter.

In our family Easter is a big holiday. I thought if we could actually bring our girls home and be able to surprise my family in Pennsylvania for Easter, it would be like hitting the lottery twice. This surprise plan of mine was a nice distraction from the anxiety caused by the e-mail warning we had received.

I called some family members in Pennsylvania to let them know we had received a date to pick up the girls. I also used the call to secretly find out where they were having Easter dinner. No one suspected anything. As far as they knew, we would be laying over in New York for just a few hours then heading home.

Later that week I went shopping to find two Easter dresses and hats for the girls.

The month of March was full of emotional ups and downs. I tried not to think of the danger we could be facing, but I am human and sometimes worry would consume me. It didn't help that our latest fingerprint scan had not cleared yet. We were told we could still go to Russia, but fingerprint clearance had to happen before our court date.

One morning while reading, I ran across this saying, "Pray twice as much as you worry and don't let Satan rob you of your joy." Worry tells God that you don't trust Him. I directed my focus on God, our new family, and our grand adventure.

One of the many things needed to be handled before we left was the business of the "orphanage donation." We had known about it since we began the process. The requested donation was $22,000.00 in cash to be handed over to our liaison, to be given directly to the orphanage. The reason they wanted cash was due to the instability of banks in Russia. Large amounts of money sometimes disappeared out of orphanage bank accounts.

We were given specific instructions about the money we would be bringing. The cash we brought with us was to be in small bills and new. New bills made it easier to spot forgery. Even though their reasoning seemed to make sense, it made us wary. What else could we do? This was how things were done in their country.

I made Jeff go to the bank to make the withdrawal. I was too afraid they would think we were up to something by our unusual request. That kind of thing doesn't bother him. He put in our request to pull money from our loan. It took a few days for them to have it ready. Silly me, I just assumed a bank would have thousands of dollars lying around in a vault somewhere. It turns out, it doesn't work that way.

Our next task was to go down town to a travel store. We purchased specialized clothing with hidden pockets sewn into the apparel. There was a wide variety of items for sale. We bought several of them. Jeff and I would split the money, each carrying $11,000.00, plus our travel money for hotels, drivers, food, and other things we might need.

Still reeling from the Embassy warning, and now having large amounts of cash strapped to different parts of my body, took my fear and anxiety to a whole new level. Even the knock at the door the night before we left, caused me to jump. I had been worried that someone might have followed Jeff home from the bank.

We opened the door to some familiar faces, and a welcome surprise. A group of friends from our church had come to pray blessings over us and our journey. This group of friends had been with us through the whole process. Over the last year and a half, they prayed for us and our future children, and often gave us a shoulder to cry on. They were with us through the ups and downs of all of it. Seeing their faces at our door was like seeing ten guardian angels.

They formed a circle and took turns praying over us. We hugged and thanked all of them. They knew we had a busy night ahead of us so they didn't stay long. We felt peace as we finished packing our bags.

"For where two or three come together in my name, there am I with them." Matthew18:20 (NIV)

Twenty-two

70 Rabbis

Once again we made the early morning trek from San Diego to Los Angeles International Airport. Our first flight took us to New York. It was now April and the weather was a bit warmer. I was recovering from yet another cold. I had had too many to count in the last few months.

As we waited at our departing gate for our flight from JFK to Moscow, I couldn't help but notice there were more than a few Orthodox Jewish men who were also waiting to board the same flight. The bearded men were dressed in the traditional garments wearing black suits and black hats. I wondered why there were so many of them traveling together, there were dozens of them. I also was curious as to why they were going to Russia, a country that had once banned religion.

The entire rear third of the airplane we were on filled up with the Jewish men. There were more than seventy of them. They sat all around us, until we were the only non-Jewish passengers in our section of the plane. A smile came over my face and peace in my heart. All I could think of was how cool it was of God to put us on this flight with these men. How could I have any fears of flying, when here we sat with God's chosen people? It was humbling to be sitting among them. I was hoping to get to talk with some of them once we were airborne.

It was a smooth take-off and soon lunch was being served. The Jewish men had arranged ahead of time with the Russian airline to have kosher meals served to them. As I glanced over at the great looking sandwiches they were being served, part of me wished I would have thought to have ordered a vegetarian meal when we booked our flight so I would not have to eat any of the mystery meat sitting on the tray in front of me.

Sometime after lunch the Jewish men suddenly all got up at once. They had arranged themselves in the aisles of the airplane. *It was mid-flight. Where could they all be going?* There weren't enough restrooms to accommodate all of them. Then I noticed the prayer books in their hands. They prayed and worshiped God right there in the aisles. I felt safer than ever!

In order to show respect I tried not to stare, but it was interesting to watch. These men would get up and pray several more times before we landed. During the flight, Jeff and I got the chance to talk with some them. They were from New York and were all training to be Rabbis. They were headed to Moscow on a missionary trip to share their faith. They were really nice and we enjoyed the time we spent with them. One of the men spoke and read fluent Russian. He was kind enough to help us fill out our declaration forms we had to present to Customs. Throughout our adoption journey God always showed up in the form of another person helping us. We were never alone, and always had help when we needed it.

The flight seemed to go quicker this time. Probably because of the new friends we made. As the plane descended, I noticed we were dropping much faster and steeper than normal. I couldn't stand it. At times it felt like it does when you are on a roller coaster. Many of the passengers were also getting nervous.

As we approached our landing site, it seemed we were still too high to land safely and not overshoot the runway. The aircraft suddenly dropped quickly. Many of us let out a scream. We hit the runway hard and bounced several times. We were going much too fast to stop safely. Our bodies leaned forward, hard pressed against the seatbelt to the point of pain, for what seemed like minutes.

Finally, we came to a stop without hitting anything. Everyone on board erupted in cheers and applause. Apparently I wasn't the only one who thought we were all going to die. I let out a sigh of relief that we had survived yet another flight on a Russian aircraft. *Only four more flights to go*. I silently wonder if we will live through our travels.

Olga and our driver were waiting at the airport to pick us up. This time they drove us to a hotel in Moscow to wait until it was time to go to the other airport. We were to wait in the hotel lobby, not a room, for several hours until they came back to retrieve us. I thought it odd that we would just sit and wait in a hotel lobby where we didn't have a reservation, but no one said anything to us while we were there, so we just acted as though we belonged.

Jeff and I kept busy doing crossword puzzles. We had picked up several crossword books at various stores when we first started our travels. We were addicted to them.

It was late afternoon when Nadia came running into the hotel lobby telling us we had to hurry and leave. The traffic was so bad in Moscow that we might miss our flight. We quickly grabbed our things and followed her out to the awaiting van.

Nadia handed us airsick bags that appeared to be from an airplane. She told us it would be best if we lay down and to use the bags if we needed them. She explained that because we were late, our driver would be driving very fast in order to get us to the airport on time. I already wasn't feeling good from the cold I was recovering from. I took her advice and immediately lay down across the bench seat. We were a bit irritated. If they knew traffic was bad this time of day, then why didn't they come earlier to get us? We didn't say anything about it. It wouldn't have done any good.

As our driver sped through the traffic jam I tried hard to be calm. I couldn't even imagine our return trip with two babies in our arms with no seatbelts or car seats to protect them. An hour and a half later we arrived at the second airport in Moscow. Thankfully, neither one of us had to use the airsick bags.

We weren't able to be dropped off at the entrance of the airport due to construction. As soon as the van pulled to a stop Nadia was out and running and we had better run too if we wanted to keep up. As we ran through the parking lot, and the black slush of what was left of winter, my lungs felt as though they were going to burst. The sickness I was recovering from had left my body weak. I was struggling to breathe as I coughed uncontrollably while trying to keep up.

My suitcase was hindering our situation. It was constantly tipping over while I dragged it across the asphalt. Nadia was in a full sprint. My lungs burned while I ran as fast as I could after her. Jeff was actually ahead of me for once.

We made it inside. We breezed through security but didn't have enough time to put our shoes back on. As we ran across the marble floors of the airport, Jeff tripped. He fell backwards to the ground, but that didn't stop his momentum as he slid across the floor on his backside for at least twelve feet. He was like a bowling ball traveling down a freshly waxed lane. He actually managed to get ahead of us by the speed at which he was traveling.

Jeff managed to pick himself up and continue running towards the awaiting airplane. We ran out the door and onto the tarmac to the shuttle. His socks were wet and black from running across the pavement. He had no choice but to put his shoes on over them.

Everyone on our flight had already boarded and was seated when we burst into the cabin huffing and puffing. I was still coughing my brains out. We had dragged our big suitcases, all of them, up the stairs of the aircraft. There wasn't time to check them. I was surprised they let us haul them onboard. The flight attendant stowed them away somewhere. The pilot had held the plane just for us.

We were met with stares of disgust by passengers as we made our way down the aisle to find our seats. We quickly sat down and soon we were airborne.

Twenty-three

No Longer Babies

Dmitry was there at the airport waiting to pick us up. It was great to see him again. Before we arrived, we had no way of knowing if he would be our driver on this trip. Seeing him was like seeing an old friend. I smiled as I watched he and Jeff hug like brothers. Dmitry didn't speak any English, and Jeff spoke almost no Russian, yet the two of them were clearly friends.

Marina, our interpreter, was waiting for us outside. She greeted us kindly as she snuffed out her cigarette. We talked a bit about the upcoming week as we headed to the car. We couldn't wait to see the girls.

Still concerned about the e-mail warning we received, I asked Dmitry, through our interpreter, how close we were to the Chechen border. His reply was, "far enough." Somehow his statement comforted me. Deep inside I felt he would protect us, no matter what.

When we arrived at the orphanage our surroundings felt familiar this time. Once again we waited in the play area for Anya's caregiver to bring her in.

When the woman came through the door carrying a child we were taken by surprise. Anya's appearance had changed since we had seen her last. Her hair had grown out and she looked older. The image of the tiny, almost bald baby, I had seen the last time was still imprinted in my mind. I hadn't thought about the fact that she would age while we were gone. Four months had made a big difference. She had gone from being a baby to a toddler. It made me sad to think we missed out on another part of her life.

At first Anya was somewhat apprehensive of us, but after some coaxing from us it didn't take long for her to relax and play. She laughed a lot...God I missed that laugh!

We played with her for a while until Nadia told us it was time to go back to the hotel. We hugged her tightly as we said goodbye. As she walked hand in hand with our interpreter back to her room, Anya turned to us while waving, and said "pa-KAH". It was the Russian word for bye. I could hardly wait for the day when I would never again have to say those words to her.

The next day we made the three hour journey to the region where Svetlana was. The drive seemed to go a little faster this time, probably because we slept for most of it. We were still adjusting to the eleven hour time change. Hopefully our hosts understood.

Even though it was still cold outside you could tell spring was arriving. There were yellow and white daffodils growing wild amongst the green grass.

While driving up the dirt road towards the baby house I spotted a babushka dressed in all black. She was carrying twigs, presumably for a fire. I couldn't imagine the harsh life she must have.

In Russia, it is not the men who are homeless, but the elderly widowed women. Their social system isn't adequate enough to care for them. The same is true for orphans. At sixteen years of age orphans are no longer cared for, and are put on the streets to fend for themselves. Their life expectancy average is twenty-three years old. Lack of food, combined with harsh winters makes it nearly impossible for them to survive on their own.

Prostitution is legal there. Many young girls turn to this occupation, or the internet, looking for men to take care of them. I wonder how many of those "Russian Brides" we see advertised on the web, were once orphans.

Svetlana's care givers were trying to teach her to walk. She was not happy about it. They suggested we try taking her for a walk outside and around the garden.

They bundled her up in full body snow suit. She had a pacifier in her mouth. Her appearance had not changed nearly as much as Anya's. She was just a little bigger than before but still sweet as ever.

Jeff and I each held her little hands as we walked her. She cried a lot. She didn't like walking, and wanted to be held, but her caregivers told us she needed to learn.

The air was cool and crisp. After a few laps around the garden I scooped her up to comfort her. It seemed to make her feel a little more secure, but she was still unhappy. It was wonderful to get to hold her again.

We stayed with her as long as we were allowed, then reluctantly headed back to town. I wanted to be able to take her with us right then, but we couldn't until after our court date, when the judge would hopefully approve their adoption. We kissed her, and prayed the next time we saw her, we would be bringing her home.

Back at the hotel we were able to keep up with e-mails by using a computer in the lobby. That is, when the server was working. Thankfully, on that particular day it happened to be working. We received an e-mail from our agency. Our fingerprints had cleared. That was cutting it close!

There were still some other things to take care of that week before we were to appear in court…

Hand carrying almost thirty thousand dollars in cash to a foreign country, and walking around with it strapped to different areas of your body for several days, was nerve-racking, not to mention uncomfortable. It was our second trip to Russia, this time to pick up our girls and make our "donation".

People often ask us how much our adoption cost. What they don't understand is that there isn't just one flat rate to adopt a child, and no one single entity gets all of the money. There were fees for everything; the agency, drivers, hotels, airline tickets, interpreters, doctors, notaries, reports, fingerprinting, passports, visas, the list seemed endless. On top of all of these expenses, there was an additional fee to be paid directly to the orphanage. This was considered to be a "donation."

Money in orphanage bank accounts sometimes mysteriously disappears in Russia, so it was required that our donation be in cash and given directly to the orphanage. The "donation" amount in our case was $22,000.00.

There were other restrictions as well. We had to take just the right amount to cover all other expenses, but at the same time could not leave Russia with more than $3,000.00 in our possession. It was the Russian government's way of keeping their economy stimulated.

The fear of being kidnapped or mugged while we were in Russia was also very real, and we were warned about it several times. Jeff and I kept the cash on us at all times, including when we were sleeping. In the event that there were a fire in the hotel and we had to evacuate quickly, we didn't want to risk losing the money. I had actually been in a hotel in New York once when the fire alarm went off in the middle of the night and we had to evacuate immediately. That memory was in the back of my mind and was part of the reason for keeping the money close by. The only time it came off was when we had to shower, and even then, it was within reaching distance. We didn't want to risk anything that would prevent us from bringing our children home.

A few days into our trip we were out running errands with Nadia. She had our driver pull the van into a parking lot. I thought maybe she was hungry and wanted to pick up some food. Once the van was parked, she asked the driver to step out. When he got out of the van she informed us that it was time to give her the money for the orphanage. *Here?! In the middle of a parking lot?!*

I wondered, why not in our hotel room where there was more privacy. We didn't question her reasons for wanting the money now. We thought she must know more about the dealings in this country than we did and had a reason for doing it then. For the most part we had grown to trust her as our advocate, but we were still apprehensive. *What if it was a set up and she was actually keeping the money?* We had assumed *we* would be giving the money directly to the orphanage director.

When she saw the look of confusion and nervousness on our faces, she happily replied, "Its okay, I give you receipt." *Like that statement was supposed to make us feel better!*

For the duration of these two trips, we had learned that things were definitely done differently in Russia than back in the U.S. Besides, we were completely at their mercy. What else could we do?

While the driver patiently waited outside, Jeff and I pulled out the cash we had been carrying from every hidden place on our bodies. We counted out $22,000, while sitting in a van in a parking lot. It felt so strange. I seriously have only seen this kind of stuff on TV.

Once the money was counted out, and safely tucked away with our coordinator, as promised, she wrote up a receipt and handed it to us. She then called the driver back in the van, and we were on our way to finish up the rest of the legalities to complete the adoption.

In one sense, I was relieved that we didn't have the stress of possibly losing the money or getting robbed. But now, there was a new uneasiness, what if the orphanage never got their money? In the end it came down to one thing, trusting the people we were working with to do the right thing.

Other business we needed to take care of that week, and much more fun, was purchasing basic necessities the girls would need for the trip home. Marina took us shopping at a store within walking distance of our hotel.

I had passed by this place every day thinking it was some sort of pizza place for children. It had a big pink elephant on the front of the building. I hadn't a clue it was a general store.

Marina and I had a nice time picking out baby food, diapers, bottles, and some toys. She was helpful in reading labels on items for me. She and I amused ourselves over the adorable baby items we found. Shopping was never one of Jeff's favorite things to do, but he went with us anyway. He probably should have stayed in the hotel. He spent almost the entire time standing around the store asking how many things I was planning on buying, all the while reminding me of the fact that we only had so much room in our suitcases. To put his complaints to rest, I put a few things back on the shelf.

Jeff and I ate dinner that night at our favorite Italian restaurant. This time the waitress produced a menu written in English. The salad was described as "green leaf lettuce topped with tongue." I decided I liked it better when I didn't know what I was ordering! Maybe this is why the Russians are not known for their food. I ordered the ravioli, trying not to think about the meat filling inside of the pasta.

After dinner Nadia and Marina prepared us for court. We were disappointed to hear they would not be allowed to accompany us into the courtroom. The law required a neutral interpreter. This was also disappointing. We had confidence in Marina's ability to interpret for us. We had grown comfortable with her. Interpreting was more than just repeating what someone says. It was also about reading someone's body language. Equally important was knowing when to leave out our nervous chatter, something that Jeff and I did a lot.

Nadia handed us a long list of questions the judge might ask us. We were to study it and have our answers ready by morning. It felt like we were cramming for finals, only a hundred times more intense.

We couldn't sleep that night. The next day would be one of the most important days of our lives.

Twenty-four

Russian Court

We arrived early in the morning at the courthouse. Dmitry and Marina went with us, but could not go inside. Nadia stayed at the hotel that day.

Outside, we were introduced to our new court appointed interpreter. She was friendly, yet professional and spoke perfect English. She wasn't as guarded as most of the people we had met. We got the impression she had been doing this a long time, and was good at what she did. After a brief meeting we felt confident about the change in interpreters and in her abilities. It was time to enter the courthouse.

We were led down a hallway into one of the courtrooms. It looked similar to the ones here in the United States, with one huge exception…in the corner next to the judge's wooden platform, was the Russian flag.

My heart went to my throat. There was no American flag, the flag that so many times had given me comfort in my freedom and rights as an American citizen. A flag that always symbolized that I was home. The reality of standing in a court of law in a foreign country took my breath away. *Would they really allow us to adopt these girls?* I hoped and prayed they would.

Something else caught my attention. The judge was a woman. Not that that was an issue, I just didn't give it much thought before this moment. In fact, all of the officials in this country we had dealt with so far were women. We discovered, generally speaking, it is the women who hold high positions of power. The irony was those same women didn't drive cars.

I was wearing a black knee length skirt, burgundy blouse and high heeled black boots. I wanted to appear conservative, yet nicely dressed for the hearing. What I didn't realize was that Jeff was wearing black pants and a burgundy dress shirt, which happen to be the exact same color as my blouse. Our interpreter, and others, asked us why we dressed like twins. I was flush with embarrassment. *Why hadn't I noticed this before we left?* I couldn't believe we had done that!

The three of us took our positions in the front row of seats before the judge, standing until we were told we could be seated. The windows on either side of the judge's platform were open, allowing fresh air and sunlight to fill the room. I needed the fresh air. I was still hot with embarrassment, and nervous to the core of my being.

The judge directed us to be seated. She called Jeff to stand first before her. Speaking to him in Russian, she asked him a series of questions about his family life, our life at home, and how we planned on raising the girls, *if* we were allowed to adopt them.

I could tell he was nervous because of how over-excited he was. And, by how he kept rambling on whenever he was asked a question. I felt for how nervous he was. I knew I would fare no better when it was my turn to speak.

Once it seemed as though he conveyed his whole life story to her, it was my turn. I stood nervously before this woman who had the power to decide if we would be allowed to raise the two girls we had fallen hopelessly in love with. I was asked about my son at home and how he felt about all of this. She also wanted to know if we felt we were given adequate time to bond with the children we would be adopting. My answer was an absolute "yes!"

When it seemed as though she was satisfied with all of the answers to her questions we were told to sit down. While the judge looked over the paperwork in front of her our interpreter whispered to us that she was surprised the judge didn't ask us more questions. I was surprised that she actually said that within earshot of the judge! The judge didn't appear to speak English, but how could we be sure? I didn't think we should be making small talk, just in case. Besides, I didn't want to be asked anymore questions.

After what seemed like a long time, Jeff and I were asked to stand. I shakily stood to my feet. I could feel Jeff trembling with excitement. The judge spoke to us as our translator translated…Svetlana and Anya would be ours!

Excitement filled the room! Jeff and I held each other and cried. There was more…the judge decided to waive the ten-day waiting period, meaning, we could pick the girls up from the orphanage as soon as we were able. Not only were we going to be a family but we would also be on the east coast in time for Easter to surprise everyone! "…*With God, all things are possible.*" Matthew 19:26

Outside the courthouse Marina was waiting for us. She congratulated us while presenting me with a bouquet of tulips. We took pictures with our new friends who helped us make it happen. It was so exciting!

We could hardly wait to get in the car and pick up the girls. When I asked when we could leave, we were told we would have to wait until the next day to get them. The six hour round trip to Svetlana's orphanage wouldn't be possible that day. We then asked if we could pick up Anya, since she was closer. The answer was a gentle no. They said it would be best if we picked up both girls on the same day. I couldn't understand why it would be better that way, but for just a little while longer, we had to do what they said. We wanted to see the girls so badly it ached.

Dmitry and Marina took us site seeing around the area. The scenery was nice and the gesture was kind, but my heart just wasn't in it. All I could think about was how early we could leave in the morning be with our girls.

That evening Jeff and I had a celebratory dinner in the hotel's restaurant. We talked about how different our lives were about to become. We joked about how it would be the last good night's sleep we would get for a long time. Sitting here, writing this book, I smile in amusement at how true that statement was.

In the restaurant we befriended a nice German couple who were also adopting. We ordered a round of beers and shared our stories. The man's name was Olaf. He designed BMW's in his country. They were fun and easy to talk to. They spoke English, which helped a lot.

When the evening was over I thought to myself about the friendships we had made during our stay there. It made me sad to think that once the adoption was complete, we would probably never see the people who helped us ever again. It was easy to form a bond with Nadia and Dmitri. They were good people, and in a sense, our lifeline while we were in their country. They had helped us so much and we would always be grateful to them.

Twenty-five

Finally!

Morning had arrived. No need for an alarm clock on this day! We popped out of bed like two kids on Christmas morning.

We dressed quickly and grabbed a diaper bag filled with some clothes for the girls. We would be picking up Svetlana first. During her adoption hearing, we were able to give her another first name of our choosing, while still keeping her birth name. From now on she would be called Haley.

There was a mix of emotions when we arrived at the baby house. On one hand, there was Jeff and I who couldn't be happier that this day had arrived, but on the other there were Haley's two caregivers, who were happy for her new life, yet sad to see her go. They had taken care of her for a long time. It was going to be hard on them. I could see the love they had for her on their faces.

It was still cold in this region. Naturally, I brought warm clothes, a sweater, a hat, and a thick coat to dress Haley. When adopted by a family, the orphanage children are not allowed to take anything with them, including clothing. It is because the little clothing they have needs to be shared with the others.

As I took her out of her orphanage clothes, I hid my shock at the extent of diaper rash on her bottom. It almost looked like it had begun to scar. The orphanages used cloth diapers due to the cost of disposable ones which they could not afford. As soon as I started to undress her, she began to cry. I quickly got her out of the diaper and applied an ointment to the rash. As I got her dressed she cried harder and harder, her face turning bright red. By the time I was finished zipping up her coat, she was in hysterics.

One of her caregivers politely motioned that I remove some of Haley's outer clothing, suggesting that she was probably too warm. As the woman helped me remove some of the clothing, Haley started to calm down and eventually stopped crying.

As her caregiver held her, I couldn't help but feel I had completely failed at my first attempt of parenting this beautiful young soul. The woman looked at me with sympathetic eyes as if to say, it will be okay, you will do fine. I wasn't so sure.

We said our goodbyes and took some pictures with them. We got in the car for our last trip across the vast countryside of Russia. Jeff sat in the front with Dmitri. He knew he didn't have a chance when it came to who was going to hold Haley for the long car ride. I held her tight as we sat in the car, hardly believing that this moment was happening. It felt strange not using a baby carrier for the ride. They didn't use them there. I was secretly glad. I wanted to hold this child in my arms for as long as I could. She settled in my arms and seemed content to be there for the duration of the trip.

The next stop was the hotel. For unknown reasons, we were not allowed to take Haley to Anya's orphanage. Nadia would babysit her in our room while we picked up Anya. We literally just got her and we were already leaving her with a sitter.

While we were in Russia things were orchestrated by our coordinator. They had a certain way of doing things to make it all run smoothly. I guess deep down we knew this, but so many times I had wanted to ask why. Once again I didn't. We were a little nervous to leave our new baby with someone, but thankfully it was Nadia. She had gotten us this far, I didn't think she would fail us.

The feelings we had when we picked up Anya were similar to a few hours ago when we picked up Haley. Pure excitement shadowed by compassion for the woman who took care of her for her short life on this planet, and who was about to never see her again. Anya was quiet while we changed her into her new outfit. I was careful not to over dress her as I had done with Haley.

Jeff graciously allowed me to be the first to hold her for her car ride back to the hotel. She seemed quite nervous. For the duration of the drive, she anxiously looked about, almost like she had never been in a car before. She probably hadn't been in a car since she was brought to the orphanage over a year ago.

Before we opened the door to the hotel room, I had Jeff take the video camera out to record the moment when two sisters would meet for the first time. Inside, Nadia was happily playing with Haley, cooing and speaking Russian to her. Haley still had the same sad look on her face she always had. Nadia told us what a sweet baby she was. She really was, it was just that everything she had known had been taken away from her.

As we introduced the two, who were now officially sisters, we didn't get the response we had hoped. They kind of ignored each other. In my mind, I had this fantasy of when they would finally meet. They would hug like little kids often do and know in their hearts that they were sisters. When this didn't happen, I could only guess, from their time in the orphanage, that they were probably used to strange kids coming and going.

If I could have seen the future I wouldn't have worried. It would take some time, but these two would become as close as sisters could ever be. One protecting the other, sharing secrets, and wanting to sleep in the same bed just so they could be close to one another.

Nadia left us alone so we could spend some time bonding as a family. We comforted the girls and tried to make them feel safe. To them we were still strangers. Anya kept busy getting into everything in the room, while Haley, still unsure of her surroundings, quietly observed her new playmate.

For dinner we ordered our favorite, pomegranate pizza, to be delivered to our room. We fed the girls their baby food and got them ready for bed. The hotel we were staying in didn't cater to families. There were only two twin beds and no crib we could rent for the night. Jeff and I pushed the beds together and placed the girls between us while we slept.

Twenty-six

Guarding Kodak

Anya and Haley were not adjusting well to their new environment. Their schedules were off and they were scared. I felt bad for them but there were still things that had to be done in order to get them back to the United States. One of those things was getting their passport photos taken.

By the time we reached the Kodak building, they were visibly upset.

Kodak and its logo had always been an American symbol of photography and fun times. It was where everyone went to get their pictures developed, before digital imaging was invented.

Nadia acted as though nothing was wrong as she walked past the man holding what appeared to be a semiautomatic rifle. He was guarding the entrance. *Why would they need guards with automatic weapons at the Kodak store?*

We slipped by the man with the gun, who allowed us passage, tightly holding the girls in our arms. We were led downstairs to a basement where there was a perfectly normal looking photography studio, another one of the many ironies we encountered on our journey. We never found out why there were men with guns upstairs.

Meanwhile, we worked feverishly to get the girls to stop crying long enough to snap a few pictures. Finally the photographer managed to get a decent shot. It was not an easy feat.

The photos were printed out in a few minutes. As I looked over the black and white prints, I felt sadness for the fear shown on their faces. If only I could reassure them that someday the fear they were feeling would be replaced with joy and happiness. Someday they would be laughing and playing with their friends, camping and swimming in the ocean. And most of all have the security of a loving family.

God probably views our lives in much of the same way. He is able to see the end result of our sufferings. He knows it will produce something joyous, even though we can't see it at the time.

Once the pictures were done we couldn't get out of that place fast enough. Our next stop was to a government building across town to have their passports made.

The traffic was heavy. There were no definitive lanes, just dozens of cars merging like cattle. Dmitry quickly darted in and out of traffic.

At one point I saw a babushka trying to cross the road. It was a suicide mission, I thought to myself. There was no way she was going to get to the other side! It was like trying to walk across a California Interstate during rush hour. She tried anyway. Dmitry didn't even slow down for her. As I yelled out in fear for her life, he nearly hit her. It was the only time on these two trips when I was really angry with him. He didn't seem to care that he almost hit her. Either that or he was just that confident in his driving abilities and knew he wouldn't. I turned my head to watch her as we passed by, wishing I had some sort of super powers to get her safely across. I kept my eyes on her until she made it, which she finally did. I felt sick to my stomach.

We arrived at an old and worn down concrete government building. It was where we would get the girls' passports. I was surprised to see it was still in use. People were milling about while others were standing in lines. It reminded me of the Department of Motor Vehicles back home. Thankfully we didn't spend as much time there as we would have at the DMV! Their passports were made on the spot. The fee was only five dollars each. Ours back home were ten times that amount! I didn't say a word as I safely tucked away the passports.

Our luggage was in the car with Dmitry. We had checked out of our hotel that morning, knowing we would have to head straight to the airport after running our errands. There would be more legal procedures to be completed once we were in Moscow, which was where we were headed next.

Dmitry drove us for the last time to the airport. Saying goodbye to him was harder this time. We knew we would probably never see him again. Facebook hadn't been invented yet, and even if it had Dmitry didn't speak English, and we didn't speak Russian. It would have been nearly impossible to communicate. Communicating in person with someone who doesn't speak your language was much easier. Laughter, music, body language, and facial expressions filled the gaps where standard communication wasn't always possible. We would miss his kind smile, but most of all his friendship.

It would be a bitter sweet departure. On one hand we were excited to bring the girls home to start our new lives together, on the other we weren't sure if we would ever be back to Russia, at least not for many years. We would probably never see Nadia and Dmitry again. We had grown close to them. They were not only wonderful people, but also our lifeline in a foreign country. We depended on them for everything. Those types of relationships usually form quick and strong bonds. I imagine they might have different feelings when couples go home with their newly adopted children. For them, the closing of an adoption might mean a job well done or a sense of closure.

One day when Nadia and I were talking, she said to me how exciting this job was for her, how she was helping so many children to find homes. Although her work is hard she truly loved it. Hard is an understatement. She and Dmitry both went above and beyond the call of duty for us, and our children, and for that we could never repay them. I hoped they would remember us.

This time there were no problems of being detained in passport control. I wondered if they left us alone because we each had small children with us. We boarded the plane without incident.

Twenty-seven

An Unwelcomed Visitor

Our first stop after landing in Moscow was to the medical center. Anya and Haley needed to be examined by an Embassy doctor before they would be allowed to leave the country.

The doctor, an older Russian gentlemen, handled our girls with a gentle understanding as they screamed their heads off while being examined. They were weighed and checked over, making sure they didn't have any communicable diseases. Vaccination records were also reviewed to make sure they were up to date.

Svetlana/Haley was now eighteen months old, and weighed a mere 16 lbs. Anya, now sixteen months old, also weighed 16 lbs. Other than both of them being underweight and both anemic, he was satisfied they could safely leave the country.

Our driver in Moscow dropped us off at our hotel. This time, during our stay in Moscow, we were in a beautiful suite at the Marriott Hotel.

Kudos to them for giving parents who were adopting children their suites at half price! It was one of their nicer hotels, complete with glass elevators. Our room was spacious and absolutely luxurious. It had a beautiful view of the city. What a nice treat after all we had been through in the last two weeks!

Someone from the hotel staff even brought up two cribs for us. There was plenty of room for them and the two queen size beds.

Anya couldn't wait to check everything out. She explored the whole room. Everything she saw was like seeing it for the first time, and it was. Haley was perfectly content to sit in Jeff's arms. We still had not seen her smile. She looked sad and lost. I hoped she would come around eventually. We would give her as much time and comfort as she needed.

Meanwhile, Anya was absolutely fascinated by looking at herself in the floor to ceiling mirrors on the closet doors. She paced back and forth in front of them trying to figure out what was going on. I'm not sure if she knew she was looking at herself.

We spent the afternoon relaxing and enjoying the children. We took them for several rides in the glass elevators just so we could hear Anya laugh every time we went up and down.

That evening we took them out for a nice dinner located in the hotel to celebrate our new family. We gave them a few small samples of different dishes along with their toddler food. They happily gobbled up everything in front of them. I am sure it was the most food they had ever seen, although at the moment it wasn't what crossed my mind. I was just happy to see them enjoying themselves and their dinner.

The girls struggled in their cribs that night. They even had trouble sleeping in our bed with us. We tried different things to help them, and us, get some sleep. We had another big day planned in the morning.

I had never been to an American Embassy before, it was exciting to me. It was also one step closer to getting our girls home. The girls and I breezed through the metal detectors at the entrance with no problems. Jeff, on the other hand, was struggling.

The embassy guards wanted to know why his backpack was setting off their alarms. I'm pretty sure they knew why, but they needed to hear it from him. They asked him repeatedly if he had any electronics in his backpack. To which he continually replied "No." This went on for quite some time. I was getting concerned they may not let him through. Finally, one of guards asked him if he had a calculator in his possession. Jeff remembered we brought a calculator to convert rubles into dollars. It ran on solar power so he didn't think of it as an electronic. I could see the frustration on the guards' faces, and some relief on their part, that Jeff obviously wasn't a threat to their national security. They let him enter.

We ended up being there longer than I thought we would. The girls were getting restless, especially Anya. I hadn't brought any food with us. Another Mom Fail on my part. Not the first, and it certainly wouldn't be the last! I gave her a bottle to try to soothe her. She started kicking and screaming. She flung the plastic bottle across the room and onto the floor where it shattered, spilling out the contents. I didn't have a sippy cup with me either.

Haley sat there in silence watching the disaster unfold. Anya's kicking and screaming continued with no way of calming her down. It wasn't like I could take her outside and get some fresh air. We were stuck there until we could obtain visas for the girls to allow them to travel to the United States. Maybe her screams sped up the process. It wasn't too much later when our paperwork was finished and we were able to leave.

After lunch our interpreter took us site seeing to Red Square, where we were able to see the famous St. Basil's Cathedral.

A couple of weeks before we left the States, Jeff, who was trying to be helpful, told me I should bring along some feminine products just in case I needed them. I was somewhat irritated that he should be informing me of this since I knew my body better than he did. I told him I would not need to take anything of that nature with me since I was not due to start my monthly cycle until we were back at home.

It was cold and gloomy out that day. The four of us were bundled in sweaters, heavy coats, boots and hats. On top of this mountain of clothing Jeff and I each had a baby carrier strapped to our bodies with the girls secured in them. We strolled around Red Square with our interpreter, learning about the history of their country. When suddenly…to my horror, I realized I had started my period, even though I wasn't supposed to for another two weeks. I hate when Jeff is right!

I spoke with our interpreter and explained my situation. She led me to a drug store which happened to be right there. I thought this was odd considering the fact this was such a historical area and the location where many battles had taken place. It didn't occur to me there would be a drug store right in the middle of such an infamous place. It turned out, this very historical place was now a shopping mall.

Our interpreter led the four of us into the drug store. Once inside, I realized just how many layers of clothes I was wearing. It was hot. We seemed to be the only customers in there. The man behind the counter gave us the typical Russian stare down while our interpreter translated the question to him as to where I would find feminine hygiene products. The man came out from behind the counter and led the five of us over to the aisle where I would find them.

Shopping for this stuff was something I usually did alone. Now, there were six of us standing there perusing the boxes of pads and tampons, while I tried to figure out which ones I would need. The packages were all written in Russian. I couldn't tell which was which, super or maxi, tampon, or pad. They all looked the same. I had to ask our interpreter to read the boxes for me. A combination of the heat in the building, along with my own humiliation, made me feel very uncomfortable.

While standing there trying to decide, I spotted a security guard by the door. He was also giving us the Russian stare down. After a few minutes of watching us he then decides to come over to find out what is going on. He doesn't say anything. He just hangs there with us, staring.

I think to myself, *are you kidding me?!!* I wondered, but didn't dare ask, if he actually thought we were going to rob the place and try to make a run for it with five people, a box of pads, and two babies in tow? So here we are…me, Jeff, the girls, our interpreter, the pharmacist, and the security guard, all standing in the aisle watching me pick out what I need for my surprise visit. I quickly grab a box, not even exactly sure of what I was buying, but would make it work. I paid for it and left the building as fast as I could. Jeff and the interpreter followed behind.

Once I got outside into the cool air I no longer felt as though I would pass out. I found a restroom, took care of business and carried on. It was definitely one of the more embarrassing moments of my life!

Twenty-eight

The Kindness of Strangers

Getting through airport security with all of our stuff and two babies was going to be a nightmare. We took the girls out of their carriers and took off our coats in order to go through the metal detector. The female transportation officer was kind enough to allow me to keep my boots on. As I carried Haley through the scanner it made a beep, alerting them to a problem. The security officer had me walk through again…same beep.

She pulled me aside to perform a pat down search on me. She had me hold my arms up in the air still holding Haley, but now she was suspended above me. The officer started with my boots and worked her way up. The room was hot and I was wearing a wool sweater. I was concentrating on not passing out while holding Haley high up in the air. I wasn't really paying much attention to what the agent was doing. Until, I felt her squeeze both of my breasts. It startled me. *Did she really just do that?!* I thought to myself. I decided it was best not to react, thinking maybe this is the way things were done in Russia.

The agent sent me through again, this time without the baby. Again, there was a beep. The agent, who did not speak English, questioned me using gestures about possible reasons for the security warning. I started to sweat. For the life of me I could not think what would be setting off the alarm.

The only thing I could think of was the hidden money belt I had at my waistline. It contained three thousand dollars in cash. It was all bills and no change. The belt was made of plastic and cloth and should not have raised any alarms, but I was so nervous I wasn't thinking straight. And in a desperate attempt to get through security I removed the money belt. I set it down and walked through. Again…it beeped. The passengers behind me were getting agitated. Finally, the agent told me to remove my boots and walk through...no beep…*Really?!*

It seemed to take forever to put all of my stuff back on. I was on the other side of the security gate putting Haley back in the baby carrier when an agent tapped me on the shoulder. As I turned around, she kindly handed me my money belt, which I had set down at least fifteen minutes before and had forgotten about! I could tell by the bulk of it that all of the money was still inside. I couldn't believe I was so absent minded as to just leave that kind of money lying around. I wanted to hug that woman! But she didn't appear to be the huggable type, so I thanked her profusely. There were at least a dozen people in that room. Anyone could have easily picked it up and no one would have noticed.

We managed to get all of our stuff together and were finally able to board the plane. Whew! The next time we stepped on land it would be on American soil!

We boarded the wide-body aircraft headed to New York. Most of the passengers on our flight appeared to be Russian, with the exception of a few American families who were also bringing their newly adopted children back to the states.

As we scanned our tickets and searched for our seats we realized we were not seated together. Jeff and Anya were on one side of the plane, Haley and I on the other. Every seat was taken and none of the flight attendants spoke English. There was no point in asking if we could move. It would be our first trip as a family, and now we weren't even sitting together.

This whole journey had been emotionally charged and I was drained. I stood in the aisle and began to cry. I wanted to be close to my new family and have all of us be together. I reluctantly took my seat as Jeff headed down the other aisle and took his.

While I was getting Haley and I settled in our seats, I noticed a man near the front who had gotten up and was speaking with the flight attendants. He seemed to be negotiating with her. I couldn't understand what they were saying and I don't know why, but I had a feeling their exchange had something to do with us. Their conversation ended and the man returned to his seat in the bulkhead area.

In a few moments, the man, his wife, and their two children got up out of their seats and headed to the back of the plane. The same flight attendant who had been speaking with the man pointed to me and called me forward. She then pointed me to the place where the man had been previously seated.

I got up with Haley and walked over to where she was pointing. There were four empty seats. It was the bulkhead area with plenty of room. There was a man seated next to one of the empty seats. He pointed to the one right next to him and offered it to me. I politely declined for fear that Haley would probably be crying through the entire flight as she had been doing most of the time since we left the orphanage. I grabbed one of the other empty seats and strapped ourselves in.

Soon after we sat down Jeff arrived with Anya and sat in the seats next to me. He too, was called forward by the same flight attendant. It was obvious, the man who was speaking to the flight attendant, must have seen what was going on when we boarded and gave up his seats for us. I cried harder. Only this time it was for the humbling kindness of complete strangers. I really wanted to thank him and his family but it was time for departure.

Once we were in the air and given the ok to remove our seatbelts, I walked towards the back of the aircraft to find the gentleman. I located him, and his family, who were all sitting separately in different areas of the plane. I approached him and began to thank him in Russian. He graciously told me there was no need to speak Russian because he spoke English. He and his wife went on to tell me they were from the Ukraine. They could tell by the situation we had just adopted the girls. He told us our new family should be together so they volunteered to move. I was overwhelmed with gratitude towards them. Giving up their bulkhead seats for an 11 hour flight, and now having their family sitting separately, was an incredibly generous thing to do for total strangers. I will never forget what they did for us that day. I made my way back to my seat and told Jeff all about the kind Ukrainian family that helped us out. He went back and thanked them as well.

It seemed that just about every child on our flight to New York were either crying or screaming. As I looked over to the man beside me who had offered us to sit next to him, I couldn't help but laugh. He was settled into a sleeping position with an eye mask over his eyes and a large bottle of what appeared to be whiskey sitting on his tray table.

It wasn't long before our girls joined the chorus of screaming babies. We had given them both pacifiers and medicine to help with any ear pain they might be experiencing, but nothing was working. I don't think ear pain had anything to do with them being upset.

They had just been taken away from everything they had ever known, had never been on an airplane, and were most likely scared to death. We were total strangers to them and didn't speak their language. My heart broke for what they were going through. We tried everything to comfort them, but the screaming just got worse.

One of the girls became combative. Tantrums went on for hours. Lunch was served to us only to have one of the trays kicked off of the tray tables sending food everywhere. I looked over helplessly at the man with the eye mask and the large bottle of alcohol. He was awake now. He looked towards me and tipped his cup as if to offer me some. I wished I could have taken him up on the offer!

After lunch the flight attendant came and whisked away the trays of uneaten food. I remember watching helplessly as she took it away. I was starving, but it was impossible to eat. With the exception of some beef jerky we had brought along, Jeff and I hadn't eaten since the day before.

Midway through our flight an attendant came over and took one of the girls from us. She didn't say anything and I didn't try to stop her. I had read previously that it was common for Russian woman to walk up and hold a stranger's baby. Russians have a kind of "It takes a village to raise a child" philosophy. At first I was nervous, but then thought, we were at 40,000 feet half way over the Atlantic, where could she go?

The flight attendant didn't speak English but she didn't need to. It seemed she understood our exhaustion and was trying to help by giving us a break. Either that or she was frustrated with my inability to calm this child down.

She took Anya and held her. She rocked her as she walked up and down the aisle of first class. I couldn't see that ever happening on a flight back in the states. Most first class passengers would never put up with a screaming baby in their area, especially if it was a baby from coach, and I couldn't blame them, though no one said a word.

It wasn't long before she brought our baby back. She wasn't any more successful at consoling this screaming child than we were. Once she was back with us, Anya had no desire to stay in our area of the aircraft. She kicked and screamed for no less than six long hours.

Meanwhile, the medicine we had given to Haley to help with the possible ear pain seemed to have revved her up. She stopped crying but would not stop moving. She was extremely restless, but we could tell she was exhausted. None of us had slept more than an hour at a time in the last 24 hours. I couldn't believe the girls held out so long.

Ten and a half hours into the flight, with a half an hour to go before landing, both girls finally fell asleep. It was the longest flight of my life.

As we approached New York's JFK airport, the four of us looked as bad as we felt. Our eyes were red and swollen. We were a mess, and the area around our seats looked as though a carnival had just blown through town. There was food, clothing, toys, and paper all over the place. We did what we could to clean up before landing.

The plane came in fast and hard. *What was it with these Russian pilots?!* We hit the runway several times. With each bump, I held Anya tighter and tighter. I started crying again. Mostly from the fear of crashing, but also from the emotional roller coaster we had been on for the last two years.

Holding her, I began sobbing uncontrollably. Our bodies pressed forward while the aircraft came to a stop. The flight attendant who was sitting in the jump seat in front of us looked at me with concern as though I might have squeezed the child to death. I made sure not to.

Jeff had Haley in his lap. His eyes were bloodshot. He looked as exhausted as I felt. We had made it. We were finally on American soil, and this time with our two daughters!

We made our way out of the aircraft and onto the jet bridge. I wanted to kiss the ground, but it was out of reach. We were immediately sent through to customs and immigration. The girls were now officially American Citizens! We picked up the rental car and made our way through New York City.

Twenty-nine

The Big Surprise

Anya and Haley were fastened in the back seat into the car seats we had rented when we picked up the car. As we drove away from the airport, I glanced back to see how they were doing. As I made eye contact with Haley, she looked up at me…and finally smiled. My heart soared!

We headed into Pennsylvania as the brilliance of the setting sun was highlighting the scattered clouds, turning them into shades of pink and purple. It was the evening before Easter Sunday.

Once we were settled in the hotel room none of us could sleep. The girls were really struggling. It had been 48 hours since they left their orphanage. They had just flown half way around the world; had already spent two nights in two different hotels, and this would be their third. They had been examined by doctors, spent hours waiting in the embassy, placed on two airplanes, gone through three airports, and were in a time zone that was 12 hours different than the one they were used to. Their sleep and eating schedules were completely off. At sixteen months old, they had already been through more than almost any kid would go through in a lifetime.

The four of us were up most of the night. I felt bad for the girls and what they were going through, but at the same time, I was super excited to be back in the states. In just a few hours we would surprise my family.

Since neither Jeff nor I could sleep, we got out of bed and got ready for the big surprise.

One of the things that most adoption books will tell you not to do is to overwhelm your new child to the barrage of relatives that will want to meet them right away. While I understand the reasons for this particular advice, I could not passed through without going to see my family while we were right there on the east coast.

It was still dark, but the girls were wide awake. I bathed them. They screamed the entire time, and continued to scream while I dressed them. I seriously wondered if they had ever had a bath. The baby house where Haley lived didn't have running water. It was possible she hadn't had a regular bath.

I felt for whoever was staying in the room next to us. Now, those people were not sleeping either. I put the girls in their new Easter dresses. Through all of the tears and screams they looked beautiful. On the other hand, Jeff and I looked like new parents often do. Our eyes were glazed over with bags underneath. We tried to smile through the exhaustion. It was now almost 72 hours since we had slept more than a couple of hours at a time. We also hadn't eaten more than a few granola bars and some beef jerky. Yes, this was definitely what new parents felt like!

The hotel was just a few miles away from my Aunt Sandy and Uncle

Lou's house. They still had no idea we were in town. We drove to their house and knocked on the door. We stood on their front porch. Jeff had a child in one arm, and a video camera in the other.

It seemed like an eternity before someone answered. My Uncle Lou opened the door. He stared, his mouth agape at the sight of us, trying to believe what he was seeing. A huge smile came over his face. It was followed by shock and amazement of the fact that we were actually standing on his front porch.

In his soft spoken sweet voice, which was filled with wonder, he said "Michelle, what are you doing here?!! I thought you were in California!" We hugged. I was so excited to have pulled this surprise off. And, I was excited to be with my family. I began trembling with excitement as tears ran down my face.

We were still standing at the front door, when at that moment, my Aunt Sandy had come around the corner from behind us. She had been visiting the neighbor. Once she spotted us, and made the connection, she staggered in the front yard with her hands to her face, screaming and crying joyfully at the sight of our new family. With a baby in my arms I ran to her. She didn't stop her joyous rant for several minutes. We stayed in the moment for a while, laughing and crying together. It was priceless, and one of many memories I will never forget.

Easter dinner would be at their home that day. Most of the extended family would be coming over to celebrate. My family is Italian, so you can imagine the amount of food that was being prepared. Giant bowls of pasta, pans of lasagna, and baskets of bread were everywhere.

None of the other relatives knew we were in town and staying for Easter. Rather than call all of them, we decided to let them show up for dinner and surprise each of them as they arrived.

Each time the doorbell rang I could hardly contain myself! The reactions varied slightly between shock and awe or utter disbelief of our presence. Tears of joy flowed like a waterfall that day as everyone met our two new family members.

Haley and Anya handled it better than expected. They seemed curious as to all of the new visitors. They got to relax and play with a bunch of their new cousins. There were kids and toys everywhere.

At the dinner table Anya and Haley sat contentedly on our laps, tasting the different foods, while Jeff and I shared the stories of our travels in Russia. They seemed to like the food we gave them much more than the toddler food we had been giving them while we traveled. We realized later they probably weren't given "baby food" as we know it. In some orphanages they are given regular food that is mashed.

That evening, and over the next couple of days we were able to visit two of their great grandmas, more cousins, and more aunts and uncles. God had given us our Easter miracle!

Thirty

Home

Goodbyes are always bittersweet. They make me sad, but at the same time, home is usually waiting on the other side.

After three days in Pennsylvania, we drove to JFK Airport in New York. While waiting to board I fed the girls some of their toddler food. They practically inhaled it so I gave them a little more. When the jars of food and snacks were emptied, they began screaming for more. We felt it best, given the large amount of food we had already fed them, not to give them anymore. The screaming got to a point where we had to find an area of the airport where they wouldn't upset the people around them. I hoped they would be alright on our next flight.

We boarded the plane and headed for home. The five hour flight was nothing compared to all of the traveling we had done in the last few weeks. The girls slept most of the way to Los Angeles. The two hour car ride home was just as quiet. They even slept through the flat tire we needed to repair along the way.

We pulled into our driveway at 3:30 in the morning.

In the darkness, we could just make out the banner our neighbors had hung on our garage door, welcoming our new family members. We couldn't wait to introduce them to our girls.

The house was dark and quiet. It had never felt so good to be home! My son was staying with his dad that night and would be coming home in the morning.

We tucked the girls into their cribs in the room they would be sharing. Jeff and I stood in the darkness with the soft glow of a nightlight, staring at them in awe as they slept. We couldn't believe there were actually babies in those cribs! Cribs that had sat empty for so long. We were exhausted but didn't want to leave their sides. Jeff and I retrieved our pillows and blankets from our room and placed them on the floor next to the cribs. We slept next to them that night.

When the sun came up in the morning, I was startled by the fact that we had not woken up at least once in the middle of the night. I thought for sure one of the girls would have cried or gotten scared. I quickly looked over into the crib. I was surprised to see both girls were sleeping peacefully. I didn't wake them; God knows they needed the rest.

Jeff went downstairs and started breakfast while I started unpacking. There was a mountain of laundry to be done.

The smell of bacon was filling the house when Sean arrived. He quickly ran up the stairs, passing up his favorite food to meet his new sisters, who were just waking up.

Anya was the first to stand up and reach out to him. He lifted her up. The two silently stared at each other. She seemed content, as though she had known all along he was her brother. Haley was awake now. Sean looked over into her crib. She was still lying down. She gazed up at him with a great big smile on her face. A smile she would wake up with for years to come. My heart was bursting with joy!

The next two weeks were filled with visits from our parents, who could not wait to meet their new grandchildren, friends, and neighbors…so much for not overwhelming our newly adopted children!

When my parents arrived, it seemed my life had come full circle. I opened the door with two babies in my arms. It was the first time I had ever seen my dad cry. They were already in love with our girls. The next week Jeff's parents flew in. They were super excited to spend time with their new grandkids and we had a wonderful visit with them.

The next most important thing happened a week after we were home...Our friends and family joined us at our church for the dedication of Anya and Haley to God our Father.

As we took the stage with our beloved pastor, I prayed that our story would inspire others, as much as the couple on this stage two years prior had inspired us.

Epilogue

We couldn't imagine what life would be like if we hadn't adopted Anya and Haley. We thank God for them.

In our hearts there is no difference between biological and adopted children. The love we feel for them is the same. I don't think people actually believe this unless they have gone through an adoption. I now understand what my friend meant when she said to me …"The children you adopt were always meant to be yours. They were just born to someone else." I believe that to be true, at least for us it is.

Jeff and I continue to relive our childhood alongside our girls. We are a family that plays together and prays together. Anya and Haley bring a tremendous amount of joy to our lives.

Every year we celebrate the day of their adoption as though it were a national holiday. We also honor their heritage and where they came from. We teach them about the culture they left behind, and the one they now embrace. They know that God has a plan for their lives. I often hear them sharing their story with others, and telling their friends that all things are possible.

Anya and Haley have a close relationship with their brothers, in spite of the age gap. It fills my heart with joy to see the five of them together laughing and joking around.

When they first came home from Russia, they adjusted well to their new surroundings. We marveled at how well they slept through the night. We were told this was "the honeymoon period." Although, it wasn't long until they were acting like normal two-year olds complete with tantrums, and everything else that two-year olds do!

Food was a noticeable issue. They could never get enough of whatever was placed in front of them. They screamed and threw tantrums as soon as their plates were empty. Even though they were quite young, not having enough while living in their orphanages had its effect on them.

In order for the girls to be healthy and gain some weight, Jeff and I educated ourselves on nutrition. During that time we learned a lot about foods and as a result, the girls now refer to me as the "health freak." Jeff, not so much. He enjoys taking the girls on occasional visits to the local taco shop, and In-N-Out Burger, which they love. Moms can't catch a break. Somebody has to be the heavy, and it's usually us!

Like most families, we have our issues. At times it has been extremely challenging. We are far from the parents we thought we would be. We yell more than we thought we would. But through it all the love we feel for each other as a family outshines the day to day issues of life. We love them more than we thought was possible. Was it all worth it? Absolutely!